Food, Farming, and Hunting

AMERICAN INDIAN CONTRIBUTIONS TO THE WORLD

Food, Farming, and Hunting

Emory Dean Keoke

Kay Marie Porterfield

Facts On File, Inc.

Food, Farming, and Hunting

Facts On File, Inc.
132 West 31st Street
New York NY 10001

Library of Congress Cataloging-in-Publication Data
Keoke, Emory Dean.
    Food, farming, and hunting / Emory Dean Keoke and Kay Marie Porterfield.
        p. cm. — (American Indian contributions to the world)
Summary: Explores Native American peoples' hunting, fishing, gathering, and farming
practices, which helped sustain early European colonists and continue to play a role in
feeding the world's population today.
Includes bibliographical references and index.
    ISBN 0-8160-5393-6
    1. Indians of North America—Hunting—Juvenile literature. 2. Indians of North
America—Agriculture—Juvenile literature. 3. Indians of North America—Food—
Juvenile literature. [1. Indians of North America—Hunting. 2. Indians of North
America—Agriculture. 3. Indians of North America—Food.] I. Porterfield, Kay Marie.
II. Title. III. Series.
E98.H8K46 2005
641.3'0089'97—dc22   2003014970

Facts On File books are available at special discounts when purchased in bulk
quantities for businesses, associations, institutions, or sales promotions.
Please call our Special Sales Department in New York at (212) 967-8800
or (800) 322-8755.

You can find Facts On File on the World Wide Web at http://www.factsonfile.com

Text design by Erika K. Arroyo
Cover design by Cathy Rincon
Maps by Sholto Ainslie

Printed in the United States of America

VB FOF 10 9 8 7 6 5 4 3 2 1

This book is printed on acid-free paper.

For our grandchildren:
Jason Keoke, Gwendolyn Z. McPherson,
Matthew Geboe, Jr., and Jonathan Ward McPherson;
and in memory of Merrill W. Bowen, Jr.

CONTENTS

⊠ *Note on Photos* ⊠

Many of the illustrations and photographs used in this book are old, historical images. The quality of the prints is not always up to current standards because in many cases the originals are from old or poor quality negatives or the originals are damaged. The content of the illustrations, however, made their inclusion important despite problems in reproduction.

AUTHORS' NOTE

At least 800 unique tribes, or bands, of Indian people lived in the Americas at the time Europeans first arrived there in 1492. A tribe is a community or group of families who share the same culture, or way of living. The things that make up a culture can range from clothing and housing styles to ways of singing or praying. They include how people make and decorate the objects they use in their daily lives. Tribal members speak the same language. Sometimes the language they speak is similar to the one that their neighbors speak. It could also be very different. A list of tribes of Indian people is located at the end of this book.

American Indians were and continue to be skilled at adapting to the places where they live. From the start the features of the land where Indian people lived and the plants and animals that they found there influenced their way of life. Their cultures were also shaped by the climate and by neighboring tribes. Tribes that lived in similar regions developed many of the same ways of doing things. For example, they used many of the same medicines and developed similar styles of art. The geographical regions where similar tribes live are called culture areas. The list of tribes at the end of the book is divided into culture areas. Maps of these culture areas are also located at the back of this book. The maps contain the names of tribes that live in these areas.

Over time tribes and their cultures change. Some of the tribes mentioned in this book existed hundreds or thousands of years ago, but they do not exist as groups today. The people themselves did not vanish. Their language changed along with their way of doing things. Sometimes they moved. Sometimes they became part of other tribes.

Other tribal groups, such as the Maya of Mesoamerica, have ancient beginnings and continue to exist today. A glossary of ancient cultures that are mentioned in this book is located on page 111. Here readers will find a short explanation of when these ancient people lived and where they lived. Maps at the end of the book show the location of these ancient peoples as well.

The authors apologize in advance for anything in this book that might offend any tribe or band of American Indians. There has been no intention to speak on behalf of any tribe or to pretend knowledge in the ways of all Indian people.

INTRODUCTION

 Indians have lived in the Americas for at least 15,000 years. Some archaeologists believe they may have come to the Americas 40,000 years ago or even earlier. Many scientists believe that the first Americans came from Asia, traveling over a land bridge. This bridge, called Beringia, emerged from the sea several times during the Ice Age to connect what is now Siberia to what is now Alaska between 13,000 and 7000 B.C. Based on new archaeological evidence, other scientists believe the first Americans may have traveled in boats as well, settling along the Alaska coastline.

By the time European conquistadores and colonizers arrived in the Americas starting in 1492, American Indians had invented sophisticated hunting and fishing technology. They gathered hundreds of plants for food, fiber, and medicine. American Indians of the Andes of South America, the Amazon Basin, Mesoamerica, and the North American Northeast invented farming independently from other people in the world. These farmers domesticated many types of plants. By careful cross-breeding and saving seeds for thousands of years, they deliberately created hundreds of varieties of potatoes, corn, beans, and other crops.

In many instances, they shared this bounty with the Europeans and taught them the best ways to farm in the Americas. In other instances, the colonizers stole seeds, which they carried throughout the world. Three-quarters of the food crops raised in the world today were first domesticated by American Indian farmers.

Indigenous people also taught Europeans how to cook the foods they grew. Colonists in New England and the Southeast learned from the Indians how to make cornbread, chowders, succotash, corn on the cob, and other dishes that became the basis of regional cuisines.

In Mesoamerica, Maya and Aztec tortillas and tamales became the basis for Mexican dishes that are popular today.

Europeans in the Americas took over American Indian farmers' fields. This was faster and easier for them than clearing land to make their own fields. In 1763 British in North America set aside land for Indians. Later the U.S. government and the Canadian government created reservations and reserves and forced Indian people to move there. Most of the land on these reservations was unsuitable for farming.

In Mesoamerica and South America, the Spaniards created the encomienda system. The Spaniards claimed ownership of the land. They forced Indians to farm it for them and to give them the crops they harvested. By the end of the 1800s most American Indians were unable to practice farming as many tribes and culture groups had done for thousands of years.

The pages that follow tell the story of American Indian hunting, fishing, gathering, and farming—a story that has all too often been forgotten or pushed into the background. The purpose of this book is to give credit to the intelligent and civilized original peoples of the Americas for their role in feeding the people of the world today.

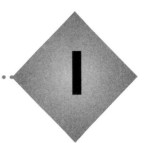

Hunting

The earliest American Indians obtained most of their food by hunting. Many archaeologists believe that they developed most of their hunting tools and technology in the Americas. They were highly skilled at finding game and killing it for food, so skilled that modern hunters still use many of the techniques these Indians invented thousands of years ago.

America's first hunters sought game in small groups or bands. Their prey included wooly mammoths, mastodons, archaic horses, and a type of bison (*Bison latifrons*) that is now extinct. Many of these animals were huge. Wooly mammoths and mastodons stood about nine feet high. The meat from one mastodon could feed a family for months. People of hunting cultures ate most parts of the animals they killed, obtaining vitamin C from organ meats, rather than plants.

HUNTING WEAPONS

The earliest weapons that American Indians developed for hunting were bolas, stone projectile points, and atlatls. Later they invented bows and arrows and blowguns.

Bolas

Hunters of the Arctic and South America used bolas to kill game. Bolas are a bundle of three or four cords tied to rocks or other weights. Throwing bolas took great skill. The hunter held a weighted cord and twirled the other weighted cords overhead. When the hunter threw the bola, the weights spun much like helicopter blades. As they hit their target, they wrapped around it. This kept the animal from escaping.

Bolas, used by South American and North American Arctic hunters, are unique to the Americas. This drawing is based on one made by Indian artist and historian Felipe Guamán Pomo de Ayala prior to A.D. 1615. (Nueva corónica y buen gobierno)

About 15,000 years ago South American hunters began making bolas by tying two or three golf ball–sized, grooved stones to leather thongs that were joined together. *Bolas,* the Spanish word for balls, was the name Spanish conquistadores gave to the weapon.

European explorers to the Arctic regions found Inuit people using a type of bola to hunt birds. The Inuit called it the *qilamitautit.* Inuit bolas contained four to eight carved ivory weights connected to a wooden handle by sinew cords about 30 inches long. These weapons could travel about 35 yards.

Projectile Points

The earliest stone projectile, or spear, points found in the Americas were made by South American hunters of Monte Verde in what is now Chile about 12,500 years ago. Some of the earliest stone spear points found so far in other parts of the Americas also date from about this time. Many archaeologists believe that Indian people shaped stone points much earlier.

Indian hunters made razor-sharp spear points from flint, obsidian, chert, or quartzite. These finely grained stones fracture easily under pressure. Paleo-Indians found deposits of this rock near the surface of the Earth. They broke chunks from it by using rocks to drive wooden wedges into natural cracks in the rock. Point makers shaped the chunks into smaller pieces and struck the smaller pieces

▲▽▲▽▲▽▲▽▲▽▲▽▲▽▲▽▲▽▲▽▲▽▲▽▲▽▲▽▲

SHARP TOOLS
Stone blades were so sharp that Aztec surgeons used them, even though they had the technology to make metal knives. The stone scalpels they used were much sharper than metal scalpels doctors use today.

▼▲▼▲▼▲▼▲▼▲▼▲▼▲▼▲▼▲▼▲▼▲▼▲▼▲▼▲▼

with an antler or bone tool to sharpen the edge. Finally they lashed them to wooden shafts or handles.

When huge game animals such as mastodon and wooly mammoth became extinct, American Indians began hunting smaller game such as bison (*Bison bison*), deer, elk, and antelope. They began making smaller points that were sturdier than the first points.

Atlatls

Indian hunters invented atlatls, or throwing boards, independently from other world people in about 10,000 to 8000 B.C. Made of a thin, flat piece of wood or antler, an atlatl had a peg or hook on one end. A hunter hooked a dart to the peg. Grasping the other end of the atlatl, he held it over his shoulder. (Most hunters were men.) With a quick forward motion of his arm, he held onto the atlatl while the dart flew through the air.

American Indians made atlatls in many sizes depending on the game they hunted. They used these powerful tools for thousands of years and were still using them at the time of contact with Europeans. The word *atlatl* comes from the Aztec language, Nahuatl. It means "water thrower." The Aztec used small atlatls to hunt water birds and fish. They also used them against the Spanish conquistadores in the 1500s. The Spaniards were afraid of the Aztec atlatls because the darts thrown using these weapons could completely penetrate metal armor.

▲▽▲▽▲▽▲▽▲▽▲▽▲▽▲▽▲▽▲▽▲▽▲▽▲▽▲▽▲

ATLATLS

An atlatl is a lever. By doubling the length of a hunter's arm an atlatl can launch a dart six times further than if it were thrown. An atlatl-launched dart has 200 times the power of a thrown dart and can reach an air speed of 100 miles per hour. Indian hunters added weights to atlatls to increase their power and to serve as silencers.

▼▲▽▲▽▲▽▲▽▲▽▲▽▲▽▲▽▲▽▲▽▲▽▲▽▲▽▲▽▼

Bows and Arrows

By 4000 to 2000 B.C., ancient hunters throughout the Americas began using bows and arrows. The bow was a long, thin piece of wood with a cord that was strung between both ends. Hunters strung this cord so tightly that the wooden piece curved, or bowed. Many North American Indians made their bows from strong, flexible hardwood saplings because they bent without breaking. In order to make the bows even more flexible, hunters rubbed the wood

△▽△▽△▽△▽△▽△▽△▽△▽△▽△▽△▽△▽△▽△▽△▽△▽△

ARROWS

American Indian hunters put feathers on the shafts of their arrows to stabilize them. Attaching pieces of two or three sturdy wing or tail feathers to the back end of the shaft kept arrows from tumbling end over end as they shot through the air. This principle is the one used on the tails of airplanes today.

▽△▽△▽△▽△▽△▽△▽△▽△▽△▽△▽△▽△▽△▽△▽△▽△▽

Indian hunters carried their arrows in quivers slung over their shoulders. This drawing of a Southeast hunter was made between 1585 and 1590 by John White. *(Library of Congress, Prints and Photographs Division [LC-USZ62-580])*

with animal fat as it dried. The bow makers used sinew, the tough fiber that holds bone to muscle, to make bowstrings. Occasionally they used intestines and rawhide. Because cord made from animals stretches in wet weather, they sometimes made bowstrings from plant fibers.

American Indians made arrows by attaching small stone points to wooden shafts that were grooved at the opposite end. They fit the grooved part of the arrow onto the bowstring, pulled it back and then released it. The sudden release of tension on the string caused the arrow to fly through the air with a great deal of force. Because bows and arrows were easier to carry than atlatls or spears, they were widely used.

Hunters of the Great Basin, Arctic, and Subarctic invented a way to make their bows even stronger than those made from saplings. They covered them with thin sheets of sinew that they bonded together. (Sinew is the strong tissue that holds muscle to bone.) American Indian tribes of the Great Basin laminated their bows by laying wet strips of deer sinew along both sides of the length of the bow. When these strips were dry, they wound more wet sinew strips around the bow across the grain of the first layer. This laminating process made the bow incredibly powerful and increased the distance from which the hunter could shoot.

Inuit people living in the Arctic and people of parts of the Subarctic region of North America used a similar process to make bows. Because trees were scarce, they used wet rawhide to hold together short pieces of wood and horns of mountain sheep and goats. After heating the horns to straighten them, they applied the rawhide in the same way that Indians of the Great Basin used sinew.

American Indians were one of only a few groups of people in the world to laminate bows.

Blowguns

Blowguns are long, hollow tubes. Hunters blow through one end of the tube in order to propel a dart at game. The Maya are believed to have invented the blowgun. The Aztec used them as well. The Aztec emperor Montezuma (Moctezuma) fired small pieces of baked clay through a blowgun for sport. Although most blowguns were made of wood, some Mesoamerican blowguns were copper.

Blowgun makers of the Amazon Basin were considered master technicians. They fitted two equal lengths of hardwood together to form the tube that would serve as the blowgun. The inside seam had to be perfectly smooth or it would skew the trajectory, or path, of the dart.

The blowguns used by Choctaw, Cherokee, and Seminole of the Southeast were about five or six feet long. Because of the blowgun's length, it bowed slightly when a hunter aimed it. Southeastern blowgun makers compensated for this bend by boring a hole with slightly upturned ends. Held in the ready position, the blowgun's bore became perfectly straight.

POWERFUL BOWS

A laminated bow could send an arrow completely through a deer at close range. Some Europeans reported that American Indians' arrows passed through bison and projected out the other side. The power of these laminated bows was comparable to the English crossbow.

CURARE

Hunters of the Amazon Basin tipped the darts for their blowguns with curare. This natural poison paralyzed its victims but did not kill them.

HUNTING TECHNIQUES

In addition to hunting tools, American Indians invented a number of effective hunting techniques. In order to lure animals and birds closer, they used calls that imitated the sounds made by game. They created decoys that looked like their intended prey. Indian hunters disguised themselves to blend in with their surroundings so that the game they hunted would not notice them. They used hunting dogs and also invented a number of styles of traps. They even used fire to move animals in the direction they wanted them to go as well as to manage the levels of game in the areas where they hunted.

Calls

Throughout the Americas, hunters saved time and energy by using calls to attract game. The most widespread call was the whistle. Hunters also made calls from sticks, antlers, and grass. Coming up with effective calls demanded keen observation. Hunters also had to find the best way to make the sound they needed to lure a particular animal or bird.

To attract female deer, hunters placed a blade of grass between their thumbs and blew over it to imitate cries made by fearful or hurt fawns. Indian hunters banged antlers together. This made much the same sound as two stags fighting over territory or a doe. Northeast hunters rolled a tube of birch bark so that one end was larger than the other. They used this megaphone to make sounds that called caribou and moose. The Shoshone people of the Great Basin region of North America banged sticks or rocks together to imitate the sound of male sheep, or rams, butting heads during mating season.

Decoys

About 3,000 years ago American Indians living in what is now Utah made duck decoys from reeds and cattails. They painted some of the decoys and covered others with the feathered skin of real ducks to make them more realistic. Some archaeologists think that ancient duck hunters of the Great Basin may have worn these decoys while they crouched under water. Breathing through hollow reeds, they grabbed ducks that came near. They also might have thrown rocks at them or netted them.

Camouflage

Sometimes American Indian hunters wanted to sneak up on game animals. At these times they used headgear, clothing, or face paint designed to help them escape detection. Throughout the Americas they used animal hides for this purpose. They also sometimes wore animal heads as headgear and painted their faces.

The Inuit of the Arctic built snow walls to use as blinds when they hunted polar bears. They hid behind these walls downwind from their prey. Their clothing, made from hides, also served to conceal that they were human. Great Basin and California hunters built pigeon blinds to catch birds. Sometimes they built them on scaffolds. Hunters waited inside of the blind and grabbed pigeons as they came to rest on it.

Sometimes hunters concealed their own scent. In the Amazon Indians rubbed themselves with the fruit of a special shrub so that animals would not detect them.

American Indian hunters from what is now Florida covered themselves with deerskins as camouflage. This engraving is based on a drawing made by Jacques Le Moyne in 1565. *(Library of Congress, Prints and Photographs Division [LC-USZ62-31871])*

Dogs

The Moche, who lived on the northern coast of Peru and the Maya of Mesoamerica, used dogs to drive deer into nets. In North America the Tlingit of the Northwest and the Penobscot of the Northeast used hunting dogs. The Yuroks of what is now California hunted rabbits and squirrels as well as larger game such as foxes, deer, and elk with trained dogs.

Traps

Natural landscape features were the first traps that American Indians used to obtain food. They herded game animals into canyons or valleys from which the animals could not escape. The Indian hunters of the Great Plains lured bison to cliffs by making the sound of a calf in trouble. Other hunters surrounded the bison and frightened them into stampeding from the cliffs; this is called a buffalo jump. Sometimes hunters set grass fires to accomplish this. The animals fell to their death and were butchered where they landed. Hunters often stationed someone at the bottom to signal when enough bison had jumped. Then they would stop frightening the bison.

Eventually Indian hunters began adding improvements to land formations. They built piled rock driving lanes that led from a natural grazing area to a cliff. The lanes helped them control the stampede's direction. Later Indian hunters studied animal behavior and made much more complicated traps. The most common were the snare, the deadfall, and the pitfall trap. They invented these traps independently from other people in the world. The Inuit of the Arctic used spring traps to kill game. The spring trap was unique to the Americas.

Traps "hunted" for Indians night and day. All they needed to do was check the traps and retrieve the animals they had caught. This freed them for other activities.

Snare Traps

Hunters throughout the Americas used the snare trap to catch deer and other game animals along the trails these animals routinely used. They made a noose at one end of a plant fiber rope. This noose was large enough to pass over an animal's head or feet and could tighten easily. They tied the other end of the rope to a tree at the height of an animal's head or put it on the ground to catch the animal's feet. Animals who walked into the trap felt the pressure of the noose.

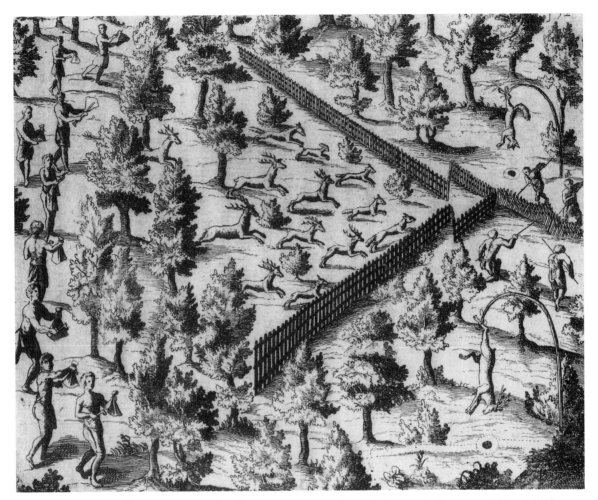

Indian hunters invented traps that would make their work easier. This picture, made between 1603 and 1615, shows hunters driving game into an enclosure. On the right a deer and a fox have been caught in snare traps. *(Library of Congress, Prints and Photographs Division [LC-USZ62-98769])*

Struggling to free themselves only tightened the noose, capturing them.

Pitfall Traps

The pitfall trap was a hole dug deep enough in the ground to prevent an animal from escaping. Hunters covered the pit with sticks and leaves so that animals would not see it. Sometimes they placed food on the middle of the covering. When an animal tried to get the food or walked across the covering, it fell into the pit.

Deadfall Traps

A deadfall trap used the same principle as a modern mousetrap. It consisted of a large weight (usually a log or a stone) and a trigger made from small pieces of wood strong enough to support the weight. The wood forming the trigger was fitted together so that it held the weight in the air. Indians baited the trigger with food. When the animal tried to eat, it sprung the trigger. This caused the weight to crash down on it. Hunters often placed deadfall traps on animal trails that led to water or natural salt licks. When an animal stepped on the trigger, the weight fell.

Spring Traps

The Inuit of the Arctic used baited spring traps to catch wolves. They rolled a strip of baleen and tied it with sinew. Baleen is the thin bone strip found in the mouths of some whales. Inuit hunters covered the coil with blubber or meat, and they left it in the snow until it froze and they could remove the sinew. They placed the trap in an area that wolves frequented and waited for one to swallow a trap. When it thawed in the wolf's stomach, the baleen uncoiled and pierced the stomach lining so the wolf would bleed to death.

Hunting with Fire

American Indians used fire to manage forests and jungles for thousands of years. Setting fire to underbrush encouraged new plant growth. This attracted game animals that ate the tender new shoots. Deer grazing in new growth produced more and healthier offspring than do other deer. Controlled burns also created open spaces in the forests. This helped hunters travel more easily and see farther.

Controlled burns over many years shaped the migratory patterns of animals. In the Missouri and Mississippi River Basins, the Indians' planned burns created more grazing area for the buffalo. By A.D. 1000 controlled burns had extended the range of the buffalo east of the Mississippi, providing Indians of the Northeast with a new food source.

▲▼▲▼▲▼▲▼▲▼▲▼▲▼▲▼▲▼▲▼▲▼▲▼▲▼▲

CONTROLLED BURNING

When Europeans set foot in North America, the land was not a wild, untended expanse. The large trees and parklike grassy areas that colonists reported in the forests of North America were a result of planned, controlled burning by Indians.

▼▲▼▲▼▲▼▲▼▲▼▲▼▲▼▲▼▲▼▲▼▲▼▲▼▲▼

BISON HUNTERS OF THE PLAINS

Although American Indians hunted many kinds of game, the bison, or buffalo (*Bison bison*) is perhaps their best-known prey. An estimated 60 to 70 million bison ranged over North America in 1492. These hoofed mammals with curved horns and shaggy brown coats roamed the continent from what is now Canada to what is now Mexico. They lived in the Northeast and the Southeast as well. The highest concentration of bison was in the Great Plains.

Indians of the Great Plains made use of every part of the bison. They used the rawhide for shields, containers, moccasin soles, ropes, boats, snowshoes, drums, and splints for fixing broken limbs. Buckskin (tanned hide) became moccasin tops, bedding, clothing, tipi covers, bags, backrests, dolls, and mittens. American Indians transformed bison horns into cups, fire carriers, spoons, headdresses, and medicines. They ate fresh and dried buffalo meat. The animal's fur was used to line moccasins, served as pillow stuffing, and was used for headdresses.

Bison sinew became glue, thread, arrow ties, and bowstrings. Plains Indians used bison fat for hair dressings, skin balm, and

In 1909, when this picture was taken in Montana, bison were rare on the plains. By 1887 white hunters had killed all but 1,000 of them to feed railroad crews or to sell their hides. *(Library of Congress, Prints and Photographs Division [LC-USZ62-91125])*

When Spaniards reintroduced the horse to the Americas, Plains Indians quickly adopted it, becoming more mobile and efficient hunters. Contrary to this 1844 engraving, based on an artwork by George Catlin, Plains Indians hunted in groups and buffalo traveled in herds. *(George Catlin, artist, McGahey, engraver/National Archives of Canada/ C-100014)*

soap. Bison bones served as sled runners, splints, scrapers, dice, shovels, arrowheads, awls, and knives. The stomach and bladder were used as containers. The paunch liner was used to wrap meat, as a canteen, and as a collapsible drinking cup. The tail became a

▲▽▲▽▲▽▲▽▲▽▲▽▲▽▲▽▲▽▲▽▲▽▲▽▲▽▲▽▲

SAVING THE BUFFALO

Today conservationists and American Indian tribes are making efforts to aid a bison comeback. Forty-two tribes belong to the Inter-Tribal Bison Cooperative. They raise bison and sell the low-fat meat to restaurants and grocery stores. Their collective herd has more than 8,000 bison.

▼▲▽▲▽▲▽▲▽▲▽▲▽▲▽▲▽▲▽▲▽▲▽▲▽▲▽▲▽▲▽

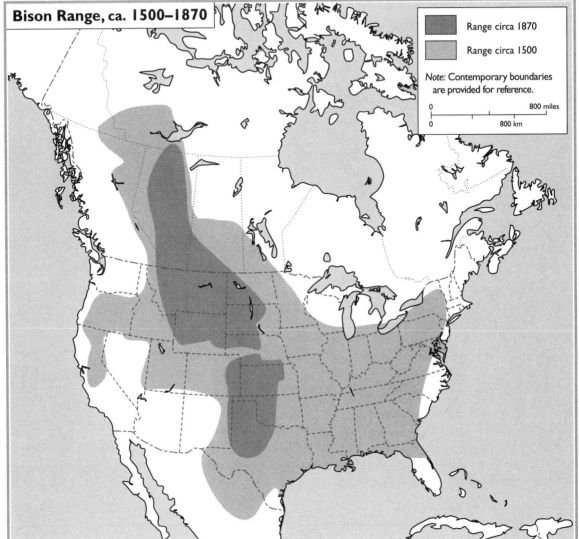

Bison Range, ca. 1500–1870

Range circa 1870

Range circa 1500

Note: Contemporary boundaries are provided for reference.

0   800 miles

0   800 km

fly swatter or a hairbrush. Indian people burned dried bison dung for fuel.

In the 1800s non-Indian adventurers began killing buffalo to supply railroad crews laying track throughout the West and to feed U.S. Army troops. When buffalo robes (skins) became a high-demand item, hunters killed thousands of buffalo a day, skinning them and leaving the carcasses to rot. A new high-powered gun also made sport hunting from trains possible; many buffalo were killed by people who never used any part of the animal. Two hundred years later, fewer than 1,000 bison remained on the Great Plains.

Bison provided food and hides for clothing and shelter, as well as many other useful items for hunting cultures of the Plains. *(Jesse Achtenberg/U.S. Fish and Wildlife Service)*

TIME LINE	
13,000 B.C.	South American Indians invent bolas.
10,500 B.C.	American Indians of North, Meso-, and South America use projectile points to hunt.
10,000 to 8000 B.C.	Indian hunters invent atlatls.
4000 to 2000 B.C.	American Indians invent bows and arrows.
1000 B.C.	Indians of the Great Basin create duck decoys.

2

Fishing

American Indians invented many tools and ways to catch fish from lakes, rivers, streams, and the ocean. They also invented special tools for hunting sea mammals such as seals and whales. The first American fishers killed fish with spears. Later they used bows and arrows for fishing as well. To fish successfully, they needed to understand the habits of fish. They also needed fast reflexes and very good aim.

FISHING TOOLS

Indians chose fishing tools that worked best in the streams, rivers, lakes, and oceans in which they fished. They also chose tools that were best suited for the fish or sea mammals they wanted to catch.

Fishhooks

Fishing with hooks that are attached to lines was often a more effective way to catch food from lakes and streams than using spears. Fishers baited their hooks with food they knew fish liked to eat and dropped them into the water.

Indian people throughout the Americas invented fishhooks independently from other people of the Americas and the world. They carved hooks from bone, ivory, antler, or wood. They made them in one piece or in two pieces that were tied together with fiber twine or with hide. About 2,000 years after South

American Indians of the Great Lakes invented copper fishhooks dating to between **5000** and **4000** B.C.
(U.S. Bureau of Ethnography)

American Indians made the first thorn fishhooks, in about 5000 to 4000 B.C. Indians of the Great Lakes area made copper fishhooks. These are the oldest metal fishhooks in the Americas. Some archaeologists believe they may have been the first in the world.

Set Lines

Indian fishers made another tool from several fishhooks and a piece of cord. They tied three or more hooks and a weight to a line. Then they baited the hooks. To cast them in the water they twirled them overhead, letting out a little bit of line at a time. They secured the free end of the cord with a rock or a piece of wood. Sometimes they tied several lines with baited hooks to a wooden bar that they weighted or set across the stream. Indian fishers could leave the stream and return to check the lines several days after they were set.

Nets

Many ancient fishers knotted or wove fishnets from plant fibers. Some fishers used small dip nets that resembled baskets. Others made larger nets. Using these big nets, they could catch many fish at one time. When they strung the nets across streams or rivers, they were free to leave the water and do other things. The nets did the fishing for them.

Fish Traps and Weirs

American Indian fishers built fish traps with stones or wood. Fish traps built from twigs and branches are called weirs. Both stone traps and weirs were like obstacle courses. Once the fish had swum into these mazes, they had a hard time leaving.

NORTH AMERICAN FISHING

Ancient fishers of North America invented many ways to fish. The food they caught in lakes, rivers, and the ocean provided excellent nutrition for their people.

Northeast and Southeast Cultures

Indians living on the East Coast built large weirs to catch ocean fish. Paleo-Indians, who lived before about 6500 B.C., made a huge fish trap from about 65,000 wooden stakes near what is now Boston,

Massachusetts. They drove the stakes into soil flooded by tidal waters. Then they wove small branches between them. The spaces between the branches trapped the fish. Weirs such as this kept fish alive and in one place so that Indians could harvest them when they needed them for food. They also caught lobsters with these traps.

The Lenni Lenape (Delaware) people ground chestnuts into small pieces and put them in streams to make fish dizzy and easier to catch. The Seminole of the Southeast used the cabbage palmetto and other plants to confuse fish. Chemicals in these plants stunned the fish without affecting the meat.

American Indians of the Great Lakes discovered unique ways to fish with nets. The Menominee and Chippewa (Anishinabe) rubbed sweet flag on their nets. They also combined sweet flag and sarsaparilla. Fish, which use their sense of smell to find food, were attracted to these scented nets. The Indians of the upper Midwest are the only people in the world known to catch fish this way.

Sometimes American Indian fishers of the Great Lakes used scent on fishing decoys, too. They made shell or wood decoys that looked

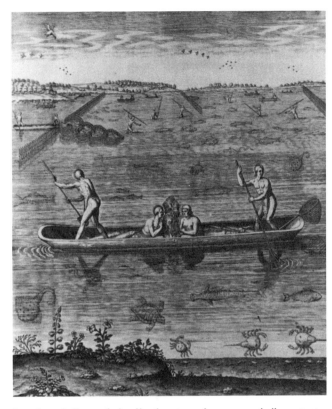

American Indians of the Northeast used spears and dip nets to catch fish. They also built elaborate fish traps, as shown in this engraving made by Theodore De Bry in the 1590s. *(Library of Congress, Prints and Photographs Division [LC-USZ62-54016])*

SEA WALLS FROM SHELLS

About 2,000 years ago, American Indians living in what is now Florida built sea walls from shells. Some archaeologists believe these walls may have served as fish traps. They think the Indian people herded the fish into these traps with canoes.

▲▼▲▼▲▼▲▼▲▼▲▼▲▼▲▼▲▼▲▼▲▼▲▼▲▼▲

FISHING SCIENCE

The Sun produces light rays that are reflected by the surface of water. These reflections make the water appear solid instead of transparent. American Indians knew that if they blocked most of the light rays from reaching the water beneath the holes they made in the ice, then the water would appear clear and they could see below its surface.

▼▲▼▲▼▲▼▲▼▲▼▲▼▲▼▲▼▲▼▲▼▲▼▲▼▲▼

like the fish they wanted to catch. Because fish travel in groups, or schools, they were attracted to these look-alikes. Indian fishers also made lures that looked like the small fish eaten by the fish they wanted to catch. They moved the decoys and lures to trick the fish into thinking they were real. The Chippewa, Menominee, Ottawa, Santee Sioux (Dakota), and Potawatomi all used decoys and lures. Often they used them in winter for ice fishing.

In winter fishers of the upper Midwest would make a hole in the ice about a foot across. Then they would build a small shelter over the hole just large enough to cover one fisher's head and shoulders. The shelter prevented the fish from seeing the human above the hole, but the fisher could see into the water. When a fish came to investigate the decoy, the fisher speared it.

Indians of the Northeast also dropped a line with a hook into the water through holes in the ice. They sat in a small shelter while they waited for the fish to bite. Centuries before this type of ice fishing became a popular sport for modern midwesterners, American Indians invented it.

Arctic and Subarctic Cultures

Since winters were so long in the North, Indians who lived there were skilled ice fishers. They used both fishhooks and spears. Their ice fishing methods were similar to those of Indians of the Northeast.

The Inuit of what are now Alaska, Greenland, and the northern part of Canada hunted seals and walrus, as well as whales. These sea mammals are very large. Seals can weigh as much as 750 pounds. Walrus range from about 900 pounds to almost two tons. Fully grown whales can be 25 feet long and weigh between 8,000 and 12,000 pounds.

To hunt sea mammals, the Inuit needed to make improvements on simple spears. When spear points were firmly attached to wooden

▲▽▲▽▲▽▲▽▲▽▲▽▲▽▲▽▲▽▲▽▲▽▲▽▲▽▲▽▲▽▲▽▲

BLUBBER
Seals, walrus, and whales are covered with a thick layer of fat beneath their skin. This blubber keeps them warm and is stored food energy. Blubber provided the Indian people of the North with a calorie-rich food source.

▽▲▽▲▽▲▽▲▽▲▽▲▽▲▽▲▽▲▽▲▽▲▽▲▽▲▽▲▽▲▽▲▽

handles, those handles often broke if the animals struggled. Wood for handles was scarce. Inuit hunters solved this problem by making heads that came apart from the handles. At first they used rawhide cord that would break for this. Later they made handles in sections with flexible joints. These handles bent rather than broke. The hunters had invented the harpoon, a tool used from Alaska to Greenland.

Hunters also made toggle harpoons. These had a long, sturdy rawhide line tied to both the point and the handle. When the animal fled, the point came away from the handle, and the hunter pulled the animal closer with the line. To make sure the point remained in the animal during this tugging hunters made barbed heads for their harpoons. Although people from other parts of the world used harpoons, only North American hunters made harpoons with detachable points.

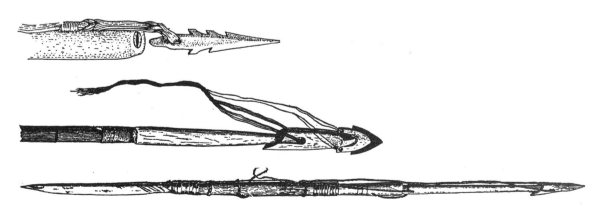

Detachable harpoon points such as these were unique to American Indian hunters. *(U.S. Bureau of Ethnography)*

Sealskin floats like the one in the foreground of this picture, tired the wounded sea mammal by making swimming more difficult. This picture was taken in 1865. *(George Simpson McTavish/National Archives of Canada/C-008160)*

FLOATS

Sealskin floats and bladders rise to the water's surface because air weighs less than water. Inuit hunters discovered that if they blew into the seal's nostrils to inflate its lungs with air, it would float and could be towed more easily. They also made air-filled, waterproof clothing to keep them afloat when their boats tipped over. These inflatable suits served as life jackets.

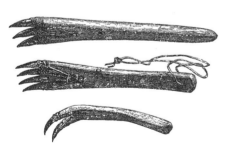

Calls carved from wood or bone
attracted curious seals so Inuit hunters
could harpoon or spear them.
(U.S. Bureau of Ethnography)

To coax a seal or walrus
back to a breathing hole it had
made in the ice, a hunter put
an ice pick into the ice and
whistled along the shaft, imi-
tating the sounds seals make.
They also made noise with a
scratcher to rouse the seal's
curiosity. When the animal
came up for air, the hunter
would harpoon it. Sometimes
hunters made this job easier
by using nets below the ice to
trap the animals.

The Inuit also hunted sea
mammals in skin boats called
umiaks. At sea they attached
seal bladders or sealskin floats
to their harpoon lines. These
marked the spot where the animal had been speared. They
also tired the injured animal
by providing resistance as it
thrashed in the water. When
the prey gave up the fight,
hunters towed it ashore with
the harpoon line.

Inuit whaling harpoons
were larger than those used for
seals. Whale hunters attached
two or more floats to each
harpoon line. They tied floats
to their boats so that they
would not tip over. When they
had paddled close to a whale,
they thrust a harpoon and
twisted it so that the point
would stay in the whale and
come off the shaft. Then they
threw the floats overboard. As

▲▼▲▼▲▼▲▼▲▼▲▼▲▼▲▼▲▼▲▼▲▼▲▼▲▼▲

NON-INDIAN WHALING

Non-Indians in the Americas did not hunt whales on a large scale until the 1600s. They used whale oil for their lamps and baleen for corset stays, hoops for skirts, and for scientific instruments. By 1924, whales had become nearly extinct. The International Whaling Commission stopped commercial whaling in 1985.

▼▲▼▲▼▲▼▲▼▲▼▲▼▲▼▲▼▲▼▲▼▲▼▲▼▲▼

the huge animal dove and resurfaced, the whalers thrust more harpoons with floats into its side. After the whale tired and died, the floats kept the animal on the water's surface. Wearing their inflatable suits, Inuit hunters butchered the whale in the water.

Whales gave Inuit people blubber, meat, oil, and bone for tools. The Inuit braided the sinew that they obtained from whales into rope and used the intestines as containers. They used baleen for traps. Baleen is the thin and flexible bone in whales' mouths that the animal uses to strain plankton (tiny sea animals) from the water.

Northwest Coast and Plateau Cultures

Hunters of the Makah and the Nootka tribes that lived along the coast of what is now British Columbia also hunted whales. Like Inuit hunters, they used detachable harpoons and sealskin floats, but these whalers went to sea in large wooden canoes. The Makah and Nootka tipped their harpoons with razor-sharp mussel shells. They added curved bone spurs to the bottom of the points.

American Indians in the Northwest and in the Plateau region depended on salmon to provide food for their people. Salmon are

▲▼▲▼▲▼▲▼▲▼▲▼▲▼▲▼▲▼▲▼▲▼▲▼▲▼▲

SALMON CONSERVATION

American Indians who harvested spawning salmon were careful to conserve this valuable resource. Even though tribes in the Northwest and Plateau regions had the ability to harvest many more fish than they could use, they understood that if they took too many, each year there would be fewer and fewer fish. Finally there would be none left, and the people would go hungry.

▼▲▼▲▼▲▼▲▼▲▼▲▼▲▼▲▼▲▼▲▼▲▼▲▼▲▼

large fish that are high in protein and unsaturated fat. These fishers used fishhooks and weirs to catch fish. They also used harpoons with small points. Often their harpoons had two or three prongs, each with a blade on it.

For Indians of the Northwest Coast and Plateau region, fishing season began in spring when salmon left the ocean and swam up freshwater rivers and streams where they spawned (laid eggs and fertilized them).

One way Northwest Coast Indians caught salmon was to make a crossbar from a piece of wood about five feet long. They weighted the bar and then hung several lines with hooks along its length. Finally they put it across a stream. They also trapped fish in nets tied to Y-shaped sticks that they dipped into streams. Sometimes they wove special baskets for this purpose. In addition, they built weirs across streams to corral the fish or to funnel them into traps.

Indian fishers of the Northwest used weirs to catch salmon. This picture was taken in British Columbia in 1866. (Frederick Dally, photographer/National Archives of Canada/C-065097)

Besides fishing for salmon, the people of the Northwest caught eulachon, a type of smelt. Herring from the sea was another food source. They also ate herring roe, or eggs. Northwest fishers discovered that if they anchored tree branches in the water where herring liked to lay their eggs, the fish would deposit their eggs on the branches. When the branches were covered with fish eggs, the Indians removed them from the water.

Plateau Indians fished for salmon in the two large rivers that would later be named the Columbia and the Frasier. They fished smaller rivers as well. Sometimes they stood in places where the water narrowed. These narrows concentrated the fish in one area so that they were easier to spear or harpoon. They also built bridges and platforms of branches over streams to better be able to spear salmon. Like fishers of the Northeast and Northwest, fishers of the Plateau Region used weirs.

California Culture

American Indians living in what is now California used substances from the roots and leaves of several plants to stun fish so that they could easily scoop them into baskets or catch them by hand. The Cahuilla people used the soap plant for this.

The Ahjumawi people, Pit River Indians who lived in what is now California, built stone traps to catch fish that spawned in lake springs. In addition to being traps, these stone mazes served as small fisheries because they provided good places for the fish to lay eggs.

CIRCUM-CARIBBEAN AND MESOAMERICAN CULTURES

As did fishers in other parts of the Americas, Indians of the Circum-Caribbean Region used fishhooks and nets as well as bows and arrows to fish.

They were experts in chemical fishing, as well. After grating a kind of wild yam, they sprinkled pieces of it in still or slow-moving water. These yams contain a substance that stuns fish. It does this by acting on their central nervous system. The confused fish could not move rapidly, so fishers scooped them into nets or baskets.

The people of the Circum-Caribbean raised fish in addition to catching them. Long before European contact, the Arawak had created large ponds where they raised fish and turtles. The underwater

▽▲▽▲▽▲▽▲▽▲▽▲▽▲▽▲▽▲▽▲▽▲▽▲▽▲▽▲▽▲▽▲

CHEMICAL FISHING

When American Indians used wild plants to stun fish, they were careful to use those whose chemicals would not affect human beings when they later ate the fish. Some varieties of yams and other plants contain poisonous chemicals called saponins. These chemicals break down red blood cells and irritate the mucous membranes. Scientists believe that cold-blooded animals such as fish are especially vulnerable to the effects of saponin.

▽▲▽▲▽▲▽▲▽▲▽▲▽▲▽▲▽▲▽▲▽▲▽▲▽▲▽▲▽▲▽▲▽

Fishers of Mesoamerica used a variety of ways to catch fish. These Talamanca Indians are shown using bows and arrows in Costa Rica in about 1939. *(Library of Congress, Prints and Photographs Division [LC-USZ62-97809])*

▲▽▲▽▲▽▲▽▲▽▲▽▲▽▲▽▲▽▲▽▲▽▲▽▲▽▲▽▲▽▲▽▲

ANCIENT AQUARIUMS
The Aztec of Mesoamerica built zoological gardens, or zoos, that contained both freshwater and saltwater ponds filled with fish. These displays were created for the education and enjoyment of visitors to the gardens.

▽▲▽▲▽▲▽▲▽▲▽▲▽▲▽▲▽▲▽▲▽▲▽▲▽▲▽▲▽▲▽▲▽

pens that they built from reeds held up to 1,000 large sea turtles. This many turtles would have provided the same amount of meat as 100 head of cattle do today.

Arawak fishers harvested turtles in a special way. They knew that the suckerfish attached itself to large fish with a suction disc in its head. First these fishers caught and fed the suckerfish. Then they trained them to be used to a thin rope fastened to their tails and gills. When the fishers saw a turtle, they released the trained suckerfish, which swam to the turtle and attached itself to the shell. The fisher would tie the line to his canoe and tow both the fish and the turtle back to shore.

Maya fishers in Mesoamerica caught both fresh and saltwater fish using nets and also hooks tied to lines. In addition to fish, they also caught and ate crabs, crayfish, turtles, frogs, shrimp, oysters and other mollusks, sharks, stingrays, and eels. The Maya used the extract of certain plants to drug the fish and make them easier to catch. The Aztec, who lived in the central part of what is now Mexico, ate fish and tadpoles (frog embryos) from rivers. From the ocean they gathered fish, sea turtles, crabs, and shellfish.

SOUTH AMERICAN TROPICAL FOREST, ANDEAN, AND CENTRAL AND SOUTHERN CULTURES

The earliest fishers of South America used many of the same tools and ways of fishing as Indians in other parts of the Americas did. In addition to making fishhooks from cactus spines and carved shells, the first South American fishers used bone tools to dig shellfish from the coastlines by the oceans. Both fish and shellfish were important

foods for these people. They later fished with weighted nets as well
as with bows and arrows for shark and smaller fish. Like fishers of
the Circum-Caribbean, American Indians living in the Amazon Basin
stunned fish by grating yams and spreading the pieces on the surface
of the water.

TIME LINE	
5000 to 3000 B.C.	American Indians of the Great Lakes begin making copper fishhooks.
4000 to 3000 B.C.	Indians of South America make fish hooks from thorns and carved shells.
4000 to 2000 B.C.	American Indians build a large fish trap near what is now Boston.
100 B.C.	Ancient fishers living in what is now Florida make sea walls that are used to trap fish.

3

Gathering

Indian people throughout the Americas gathered seeds, picked fruits, and dug the roots of plants for food. These gatherers collected thousands of kinds of wild plants for food. Some of these foods are eaten throughout the world today. Other plant foods of ancient American gatherers are not so widely known outside of the tribes that originally ate them.

American Indians also gathered plants for fibers to make clothing, houses, and ropes. Indian people used some of the plants they gathered for dye to color fabric and even food. They also used wild plants for medicines.

WELL-KNOWN FOODS THAT NORTH AMERICAN INDIANS GATHERED

Many of the foods American Indians first gathered have become part of the diet of people throughout the world today.

PLANTS AS FOOD AND MEDICINE

Some of the plants that Indian people gathered were used both as food and medicine. Cranberries eaten by the Indians who lived in what is now New England contain high amounts of vitamin C. The vitamin C in cranberries helped the Indians who ate them avoid scurvy. Scurvy is a disease that causes sore joints, loose teeth, and slows healing for cuts and bruises. It is caused by taking in too little vitamin C and can eventually end in death.

Blackberries

Blackberries are the fruits from a prickly bush. These fruits are made up of a number of smaller black or dark red seeded fruits. Indians of the North American Subarctic and Northeast cultures, including the Potawatomi and the Mohawk, gathered blackberries. They ate them fresh or dried them for winter storage. Some North American tribes used blackberries as medicine. European settlers used blackberries that grew in North America for jams, jellies, vinegar, and brandy.

Black Walnuts

Black walnuts grow on trees that are native to parts of North America. The nuts are covered with a green husk about the size of a golf ball. Indians throughout North America shelled and ate the nuts. Eastern Woodland Indian people used crushed nutmeats and black walnut oil in cornbread and pudding. Great Plains Indians ground walnuts and made them into soup or ate them with honey.

Indians from many tribes used the outside husk that turns black once the nut falls from the tree as a dye and to tan leather. Some California Indians used the nutshells for gambling games. Today black walnuts are a popular ingredient in candy and ice cream throughout the world. The black walnut tree produces a hardwood that is valued by modern woodworkers for fine furniture making and other projects.

Blueberries

Blueberries are small, sweet fruits that grow on bushes. Blueberries contain high levels of vitamins A, C, and E. They also contain antioxidants, chemicals that neutralize free radicals, which scientists believe may play a role in cancer and aging. American Indians living in the Northeast and the Great Plains added dried or fresh blueberries to soups and stews. The French explorer Samuel de Champlain reported in the early 1600s that Indians living near what is now called Lake Huron made blueberry pudding. They

TODAY'S BLUEBERRIES

Blueberries grow throughout the world, but the wild highbush blueberry is the type grown commercially in the United States. It is the same kind that American Indians gathered. Today farmers in 30 states grow blueberries. Half of those blueberries are made into jams, pies, and other baked goods.

Blueberries remain a part of traditional American Indian cooking in regions of North America where they grow. This picture of a woman picking blueberries was taken near Little Fork, Minnesota, in 1944. Little Fork is near the Bois Forte Chippewa Reservation in northern Minnesota. *(Library of Congress, Prints and Photographs Division [LC-USF33-011262-M1])*

mixed powdered, dried berries with water, cornmeal, and wild honey.

Indians taught the English settlers how to dry blueberries. Later explorers Lewis and Clark relied on pemmican, an Indian food made from dried berries—often blueberries—and dried meat on their journey to the Northwest.

Cranberries

Cranberries are the tart fruit that grows on bushes in the northern United States and lower Canada. American Indians mashed and mixed them with dried deer meat to make pemmican. Indians of the Northwest mixed cranberries with crab apples to make a drink similar to today's cranberry juice cocktail. Arctic Indians mixed them with blubber for a frozen dessert that was high in vitamin C.

▲▽▲▽▲▽▲▽▲▽▲▽▲▽▲▽▲▽▲▽▲▽▲▽▲▽▲

OTHER USES FOR CRANBERRIES
Indians of many tribes used cranberries to dye blankets, clothing, and rugs. They also used cranberries for medicines. The Lenni Lenape (Delaware) Indians, who lived in what is now New Jersey, believed the berries were so important that they used the cranberry as a symbol of peace.

▽▲▽▲▽▲▽▲▽▲▽▲▽▲▽▲▽▲▽▲▽▲▽▲▽▲▽

German and Dutch settlers to the Americas called the fruits "crane berries." (A crane is a kind of large bird.) They thought cranberry blossoms looked like a crane's neck, head, and bill. They gathered cranberries but did not cultivate them until 1816.

Grapes

Grapes are small, sweet fruits that grow on vines. American Indians who lived where grapes grew wild used them for food. Although grapes also grew in Europe, the muscadine and scuppernong grapes that Indians gathered and ate impressed explorers. Giovanni de Verrazano, the Italian navigator who explored what is now the Cape Fear River Valley in North Carolina in 1524 wrote in his logbook: "Grapes of such greatness, yet wild, as France, Spain, nor Italy hath no greater." American Indians also ate rock grapes and Oregon grapes.

Maple

Maple sap comes from sugar maple trees that are native to the Northeast of North America. American Indians collected this sap and drank it. They also boiled it to make maple syrup and maple sugar to sweeten their food. Maple syrup and sugar gave them quick energy. Unlike refined sugar, maple syrup contains the minerals calcium, potassium, phosphorus, manganese, magnesium, and iron.

To gather maple sap, in springtime Indians made V-shaped cuts in the trees. Then they inserted reeds or pieces of bark for taps. They collected the sap in birch-bark buckets. A great deal of sap was needed to make syrup. During an entire sugaring season one tree produces from 35 to 50 quarts of sap. On a warm day a birch-bark pail might fill in an hour. When it is boiled, this amount makes a quart to a quart and a half of maple syrup. Sugaring was a busy time because the Indians tapped hundreds of trees.

When they had collected enough sap, they concentrated the sap into syrup. One way they did this was to drop hot stones into

This engraving made in 1724 shows American Indians collecting sap from maple trees and boiling it. Before contact with Europeans, Indians boiled the sap by dropping hot rocks into stone or wooden containers. *(Library of Congress, Prints and Photographs Division [LC-USZ62-98722])*

MAPLE SAP

Maple sugaring season lasted several weeks. This time was so important to the Chippewa (Anishinabe), a tribe of the upper Midwest, they named a month after it—*Slzhkigamisegi Geezis*, which means "moon of boiling." Algonquian speakers, who lived along the St. Lawrence River, called maple syrup *sinzibuckwud*, which means "drawn from wood."

American Indians of the Northeast gathered maple sap in birch-bark buckets. *(Library of Congress, Prints and Photographs Division [LC-USZ62-105740])*

wooden bowls containing sap. Another way was to freeze the sap and get rid of the ice that formed at the top. This ice was mostly water. To make sugar, Indian people boiled sap until it was thick, then poured it onto snow to harden. They tightly packed this hardened syrup in birch-bark cones and sewed the tops shut to store it.

The Indian people of the Northeast taught American colonists how to tap trees and make syrup and sugar. Early colonial land sellers encouraged Europeans to cross the ocean by telling them that they could grow their own sugar in America.

▲▽▲▽▲▽▲▽▲▽▲▽▲▽▲▽▲▽▲▽▲▽▲▽▲▽▲

MAPLE SUGAR

The Chippewa (Anishinabe) made granulated sugar by dropping pieces of deer tallow into the syrup. Just before the sugar began to granulate, they poured it into wooden troughs and rubbed it with wooden ladles or with their hands to make grains. They then poured it into birch-bark containers or rawhide bags. They used this sugar throughout the year to season fruit, vegetables, corn, meat, and fish. They also used it to sweeten herbal teas, and they added it to water to make a sweet drink.

▽▲▽▲▽▲▽▲▽▲▽▲▽▲▽▲▽▲▽▲▽▲▽▲▽▲▽

Mints

Mints are plants that contain a strong-smelling oil in their stems and leaves. This oil also has a pleasant taste. Many tribes of American Indians gathered several types of mint that grow wild in North America. They used dried and crumbled mint leaves to season food, especially meat. Sometimes American Indians chewed mint leaves for the refreshing taste they provided. They also used mint to make tea.

Persimmons

Persimmons are trees that produce a small, round, dark red-orange fruit. This fruit is sweet when it is ripe. It is high in vitamin C and vitamin A. American Indians of the Northeast and the Southeast ate wild persimmons and made them into drinks. Often they dried them in order to preserve them throughout the winter.

Ripe persimmons are found in grocery stores today. Because they are soft and do not ship well, they are a seasonal item.

The word *persimmon* comes from the Cree word *pasimian,* which means "dried fruit." The Cree is a tribe of the upper Midwest.

Prickly Pear Cactus

Prickly pear cactus grows in the Southwest desert of the United States and northern Mexico. It has flat stems called pads. They are topped with flowers in the spring. These flowers turn into fruits, or tunas, in the summer. Even in very dry summers this cactus produces juicy, sweet fruits.

Fruits of the prickly pear cactus were an important part of the diet of Indians of the desert Southwest. *(Gary M. Stoltz/U.S. National Fish and Wildlife Service)*

The cactus was a plentiful and easy-to-gather source of food for the ancient Anasazi of the Southwest as well as the Aztec of Mesoamerica. One person was able to gather 19 pounds of fruit in 20 minutes. Not all of the tunas needed to be gathered at once. Left on the cactus plant, the tunas could be picked and eaten well into the winter. American Indians of the Southwest and the Aztec removed the spines from cactus pads and ate them roasted, boiled, or raw. The Aztec boiled the juice of sweet tunas to make sugar. Today prickly pear tunas and pads are a part of southwestern cooking and are sold in many Mexican grocery stores. The pickled pads are called *nopales* or *nopalitas*.

Strawberries

Strawberries grow close to the ground and reproduce by sending out runners. The red fruits have their seeds on the outside. Just eight strawberries contain 140 percent of the daily requirement for vitamin C. American Indians of the Northeast mashed strawberries and

△▽△▽△▽△▽△▽△▽△▽△▽△▽△▽△▽△▽△▽△▽△▽△▽

SHORTCAKE

Indians of the Northeast pounded fresh strawberries and mixed them with cornmeal to make a type of strawberry bread. Colonists enjoyed this desert so much that they began making it, substituting wheat flour for cornmeal. Strawberry shortcake is still popular today.

▽△▽△▽△▽△▽△▽△▽△▽△▽△▽△▽△▽△▽△▽△▽△▽△▽

combined them with water to make a drink. Often Indian people mixed dried strawberries with dried, pounded meat and animal fat, making pemmican.

Strawberries are now one of the most popular small fruits grown in North America. Farmers in every state in the United States and in every Canadian province grow them. Modern plants were developed by crossbreeding both North and South American strawberry plants with those native to Europe.

Wild Rice

Wild rice is a seed-bearing plant that grows about eight to 12 feet tall. It grows in water that is three to eight feet deep. American Indians who lived in the upper Great Lakes region, including the Chippewa (Anishinabe), Assiniboine, and Potawatomi, depended on wild rice for food.

Women, who were responsible for gathering the rice, took canoes into the water and tied rice stalks into bundles. About two weeks later, when the rice was ripe, they cut these sheaves. In camp they knocked the rice grains from the sheaves. Some of this rice, called green rice, was eaten right away. They dried most of the rice that they had gathered in the sun or on a frame made of green branches over a low fire.

When it was dry, the Indians heated the rice over a fire so that the husks would come off more easily. This also gave the rice a different taste than that of green rice. When they had parched the rice, they put it in a wooden container and gently pounded on it with long-handled wooden poles to remove the husks. Indian women placed the rice in birch-bark trays and tossed it into the air so that

> The Chippewa (Anishinabe) called wild rice *manomin,* or "good berry." The first part of the word, *Manido,* is the spirit giver whom the Chippewa believe brought rice to the people. French voyagers later called the rice *folle avenoine,* or wild oats.

▲▽▲▽▲▽▲▽▲▽▲▽▲▽▲▽▲▽▲▽▲▽▲▽▲▽▲▽▲

SAVING WILD RICE FROM EXTINCTION

In the 1960s non-Indians discovered a market for wild rice as a gourmet food item. They began harvesting it in flat-bottom wooden boats that crushed the plants. Because they harvested every bit of rice they could, they left only a few seeds behind to grow more plants. Today the White Earth Band of Chippewa (Anishinabe) responsibly harvests and sells wild rice. They do this to keep their gathering tradition alive and to raise money for the tribe's land recovery project.

▽▲▽▲▽▲▽▲▽▲▽▲▽▲▽▲▽▲▽▲▽▲▽▲▽▲▽▲▽

The Anishinabe women in this watercolor made in 1867 by Seth Eastman harvested wild rice by beating the stalks with paddles to loosen the grains. *(Stock Montage/The Newberry Library)*

the husks would blow away. Finally they hung the winnowed rice grains in a skin bag over a fire in order to dry them further.

Wild rice was such an important source of food that centuries ago American Indian rice harvesters began planting it. They scattered seeds for as much as a third of the crop that they harvested from marshes. The Assiniboine people weeded their wild rice fields.

WELL-KNOWN FOODS THAT MESOAMERICAN AND SOUTH AMERICAN INDIANS GATHERED
Blue-Green Algae

Blue-green algae are tiny water plants with no stems or leaves. Blue-green algae are high in chlorophyll. They were an important food for the Aztec, who skimmed them from lakes in the Valley of Mexico with nets or shovels. The Aztec then sun-dried the algae and cut the dried algae into bricks. Preserved in this way they remained good to eat for a year.

The Aztec combined algae with tortillas, chili peppers, or tomatoes. Some of the Spanish conquistadores referred to blue-green algae as slime, and most refused to eat the food. After the Spanish defeated the Aztec, they drained the lakes in the Valley of Mexico. American Indians were no longer able to grow algae. Rediscovered in the 1970s, blue-green algae is sold as a high-protein health food today.

Brazil Nuts

Brazil nuts grow on huge rain forest trees native to the Amazon Basin. The trees grow as tall as 160 feet. Twelve to 25 Brazil nuts are arranged inside hard, woody pods that drop to the ground when they are ripe. The nuts are high in protein and fat.

Indian people living in the tropical forests of South America ate Brazil nuts raw. Sometimes they grated them and cooked them. They removed the oil from Brazil nuts to use as fuel for cooking and in lamps. American Indians also used wood from Brazil nut trees for houses. They used empty seedpods to hold latex they gathered from rubber trees.

Dutch traders began exporting the nuts in about 1600. Today Brazil nuts are second only to rubber as a Brazilian export. People throughout the world eat them. Oil from the nuts is used in shampoo, skin creams, and hair conditioner.

Cashews

Cashews grow on trees native to what are now Mexico, Brazil, Peru, and the West Indies. The nuts are high in protein and fat. They are also high in vitamin A, calcium, phosphorus, iron, and fiber. In addition to eating the cashew's nuts, the people of South America gathered and ate the apple-like fruit that surrounds the nut. The Cuna Indians, living in what is now Brazil, used cashew bark and leaves for medicine. American Indians in the Amazon Basin used cashew wood to build their homes because it repelled insects.

The Portuguese took trees to their colonies in East Africa, India, and Indonesia. Today people throughout the world enjoy cashews. The clear, sticky liquid from the stems of the fruit is used to make pills. Cashew nut shell liquid, or CNSL, a by-product of cashew processing, is used to waterproof and protect wood from termites. CNSL dust is used for brake linings and clutch facings in cars. Cashew juice, which turns black when exposed to the air, makes indelible ink.

OTHER FOODS
THAT AMERICAN INDIAN PEOPLE GATHERED

From wild onions and morel mushrooms to tree buds and more than 50 kinds of seed grasses, Indian people of the Americas gathered plants that provided them with a varied diet. Many of these plants are not familiar to non-Indians today and can easily be confused with plants that are poisonous. Indians knew what was safe to eat because they experimented over time and remembered which plants were harmful and which were safe to eat.

Cattails

Cattails are marsh plants that grow throughout many parts of North America. They have tall stalks topped by cylinder-shaped heads that are covered with tiny brown flowers. American Indians of the Northeast began gathering cattails thousands of years ago. Because cattails contain 10 times as much starch as potatoes, they were a good source of food energy. Indians picked and peeled cattail shoots in the springtime. In the winter, they dried the roots and pounded them into flour. Cattails were used as medicine and for making mats and baskets.

Fruits and Berries

Fruits are the ripened ovaries of flowers. Berries are fleshy fruits with more than one seed. Indians of North America gathered chokecherries and wild plums, huckleberries, buffalo berries, and service berries. They ate them fresh in the summer and dried them for winter eating. North American Indians also gathered wild rose hips. These are a very good source of vitamin C. Mesoamerican and Amazon Basin Indians also gathered wild guava and other tropical fruits.

Leafy Green Vegetables

Leafy green vegetables are high in vitamins A and C as well as calcium, iron, and fiber. Indians of all culture groups ate green vegetables both cooked and in salads. American Indians of the Northeast, Southeast, and Northwest boiled young ferns. Some other plants that North American Indians ate were dandelion, dock, wild mustard, and miners' lettuce. Indians of Mesoamerica and South America ate wild amaranth leaves. Some of these plants are considered weeds today, but they were valuable sources of nutrition for ancient peoples.

Milkweed

Milkweed is a flowering plant that contains a white, sticky substance called latex. Many Indians in North America ate milkweed seed pods, shoots, and flowers. They used the plant for medicine and made fishing nets and ropes from milkweed fibers. Some Indians used milkweed latex as a dye. North American Indians used the milky white sap of the milkweed plant as chewing gum and a breath freshener. European colonists eventually picked up this habit. The fluff from milkweed became a disposable diaper used to line cradle boards (baby carriers).

Nuts

Nuts are fruits with hard shells around a kernel. Indians of the Southwest gathered piñon nuts from pine trees. In addition to hickory nuts and pecans, which they later domesticated, North American Indians ate acorns. Indigenous people living in what is now California depended on acorns for food. Acorns contain tannic acid, which makes them poisonous and bitter. American Indians removed this acid from acorns. They crushed acorn nutmeats and put them into a hole that they had dug in wet sand. Over several hours they poured water into the hole. The tannic acid drained from the nutmeats into the sand, and the acorns were safe to eat.

Roots and Tubers

Roots and tubers are the parts of plants that grow underground. (Tubers are swollen underground stems.) The nutrition they provide is in the form of starch, a carbohydrate that fuels the body with energy. North American Indians ate roots and tubers that included prairie turnip, camas, and yampa, among others. American Indians of the desert Southwest ate wild potatoes as did Indians of South America. Indians of the Amazon Basin and the Circum-Caribbean gathered wild manioc roots.

Ancient Farming

 Three of every four varieties of food crops grown throughout the world today are native to the Americas. Long before contact with Europeans, American Indian farmers domesticated most of these crops from the wild plants they gathered. Foods that American Indians raised include corn, potatoes, beans, and tomatoes—just to name a few. Besides growing food crops, indigenous farmers grew plants for medicine, dyes, and fiber used to make clothing, ropes, and other useful items.

American Indian farmers grew cacao trees and harvested the pods to make chocolate. They invented corn that popped when exposed to heat. From peanuts and pecans to pineapple, many of the foods eaten today would not be on people's plates were it not for hundreds of years of work on the part of American Indian farmers.

In addition to developing more than 300 species and thousands of varieties of crops, American Indians invented farming techniques that were suited to the land and climate where they lived. European colonists found that their own farming methods did not work well in

PLANT SPECIES AND VARIETIES

A species is a group of plants or animals that shares common characteristics. A variety is a smaller group of plants within a species. The kinds of plants that make up a variety have genetic differences from other varieties of plants within the species. They show genetic similarities to each other.

the Americas. The agricultural knowledge American Indians shared helped them to survive. Many of the methods that Indian farmers invented are still used by today's gardeners—especially organic gardeners, those who grow crops without using chemicals to kill weeds and insects.

THE BIRTH OF AGRICULTURE

Since they were familiar with plants as a result of gathering, American Indian women were probably the first farmers. Anthropologists, scientists who study human cultures, do not know the exact steps these women took to move from gathering food to planting and harvesting crops. It could have happened in a number of ways. The most commonly accepted theory is that women carrying seeds home for their families dropped some of them on the ground.

The women noticed that the fallen seeds turned into plants, and they began deliberately scattering more seeds closer to their villages. The act of planting greatly improved their odds of finding food. They did not have to look so hard to find food and did not have to walk so far to gather it.

As women observed their work, they saw that plants grew faster and larger from seeds that they had dropped on refuse piles, or middens. The soil there was rich, much like that in a compost pile. (Compost is rotted organic material that provides nutrients for plants.) They noticed that the seeds they sowed on soft, moist ground that had been disturbed were more likely to sprout than seeds that they sowed on hard, dry ground. When they pulled weeds in these early gardens, the plants they grew were sturdier. The women studied how much sunlight the plants needed and how much water. They learned the best time of year to plant seeds and the types of soil in which certain plants grew best.

This increasing knowledge gave them the skills to produce more and better food crops. As each generation of women experimented and learned more about growing food, they taught their daughters and granddaughters what they had discovered.

AN AGRICULTURAL REVOLUTION

Farming not only changed what people in the Americas ate, it changed how they lived. At first, planting did not replace gathering as a way to obtain food, but after hundreds of years and many

▲▽

AN INDIAN FARMER REMEMBERS

Buffalo Bird Woman, or Maxidiwiac in the Hidatsa language, was born in about 1839. She shared what she knew about the farming ways of her tribe, the Hidatsa, with historian Gordon Wilson, telling him how her grandmother Turtle made a garden in the lowlands by North Dakota's Knife River.

Turtle used a digging stick made of ash tree wood to loosen the soil for planting. Her hoe was an animal's shoulder bone tied to a wooden handle with a piece of leather. She made a rake by fastening a black-tailed deer antler to a stick with a leather thong.

"I was six years old then, I think, quite too little to help her any, but I liked to watch my grandmother work," Buffalo Bird Woman remembered. "With her digging stick, she dug up a little round place . . . I remember seeing my grandmother digging along the garden with her digging stick, to enlarge the field and make the edges even and straight."

Her methods were the same as those of the Indian women who had farmed for thousands of years throughout the Americas.

Wilson made Buffalo Bird Woman's conversations about Hidatsa farming techniques into a book. *Buffalo Bird Woman's Garden* was first published in 1917.

This Hidatsa woman hoed squash with her bone hoe in this picture taken in 1912. She used the farming methods described by Buffalo Bird Woman. *(Gilbert Wilson, photographer/Minnesota Historical Society)*

▽▲

generations of experimenting, America's first farmers gained more control of food production. Eventually they were able to increase the food supply so much that agriculture became a full-time job for them.

Because by then women were growing many crops that produced higher and higher yields, men began helping them to clear trees and brush from more land in order to create more fields for crops. As agriculture gained in importance, it was not necessary for the men to spend so much time hunting.

Groups of people who planted and harvested no longer had to move their temporary villages from place to place to search for food. They needed to stay by their fields in order to tend their crops, so they built more permanent villages. Because agriculture did not take as much time as hunting and gathering, they were able to spend more time on other tasks such as making baskets and pottery. In addition to finding new ways to make everyday objects, they began creating art.

The ability of early American farmers to consistently feed many more people than they could by hunting and gathering also meant that more people could live in one place than ever before. As a result, villages grew in size. Eventually some of them became cities.

Societies made up of many people who lived close together needed governments to maintain order. The Maya and Aztec societies in Mesoamerica were based on agriculture, as was the Inca Empire, which arose in South America. Maya culture arose in about 1500 B.C. The Aztec Empire was established in about A.D. 1100. The Inca established their empire in about A.D. 1000. In North America's Northeast the Iroquois League was made up of the Mohawk, Oneida, Onondaga, Cayuga, and Seneca tribes between A.D. 1100 and A.D. 1450. All of these tribes were agricultural.

PLACES WHERE FARMING FIRST BEGAN

America's first farmers began domesticating, or taming, plants at least 10,000 years ago. Some researchers think they may have farmed even earlier than this. For years archaeologists, scientists who study the past, believed that farming was invented in only one place in the Americas—the Tehuacán Valley in the central part of what is now Mexico. They believed that all of the agriculture in the Americas had been spread from this one region.

> Although Indian people living in what are now New Mexico and Arizona were excellent farmers, these people of the Southwest learned farming from their neighbors to the south. They did not invent it independently.

Although they found seeds stored in caves and in grass-lined storage pits at ancient sites in the Northeast of North America, most archaeologists guessed that they had been gathered. They saved them but did not closely examine them. In the mid-1980s a scientist decided to look at the old seeds with a new tool, the scanning electron microscope.

What he saw showed that ancient Indians of the Northeast had taught themselves to cultivate at least four food crops on their own with no help from the Mesoamerican farmers. Once archaeologists were certain that agriculture arose in two places in the Americas, many more of them became interested in finding the roots of the earliest American Indian agriculture. The more places they looked for signs of independent crop domestication, the more evidence they found.

Currently scientists are certain that at least four different groups of ancient Americans independently invented farming. In addition to the people of the Tehuacán Valley and those of the Northeast, people living in what are now the South Central Andes of Peru learned how to farm on their own. By the year 2000, scientists had learned that people living in what is now the Amazon River Basin of Brazil also independently invented agriculture.

▲▽▲▽▲▽▲▽▲▽▲▽▲▽▲▽▲▽▲▽▲▽▲▽▲▽▲▽▲▽▲

HOW CAN SCIENTISTS TELL WHERE AGRICULTURE BEGAN?

The hard coats that cover seeds are thinner in domesticated plants (those grown by farmers) than they are in wild plants. Scientists study seeds found at sites where people lived thousands of years ago under an electron microscope in order to measure the thickness of the seeds' coats. Then they compare them to seeds grown in nature without human help.

Today, scientists can also trace variations in the genes of plant remains that they find at sites where ancient people lived. They compare the remains with those of wild plants. By constructing a crop's "family tree" based on the presence of a single gene, scientists gain important clues about where a plant was first domesticated.

▽▲▽▲▽▲▽▲▽▲▽▲▽▲▽▲▽▲▽▲▽▲▽▲▽▲▽▲▽▲▽

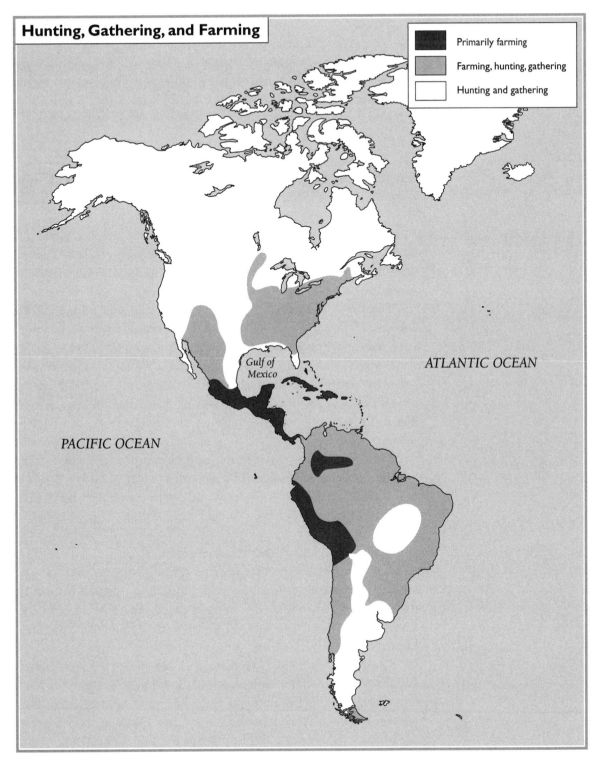

Hunting, Gathering, and Farming

Primarily farming

Farming, hunting, gathering

Hunting and gathering

ATLANTIC OCEAN

PACIFIC OCEAN

Gulf of Mexico

Many scientists believe that the invention of farming in the Americas was even more widespread. They are studying plants and ancient plant remains on the coast of what is now Ecuador, in Colombia, and in Belize, as well as in the central part of what is now Panama and in the northern part of what is now Peru. Perhaps some of these sites will also prove to be birthplaces of American Indian agriculture.

THE FIRST AMERICAN FARMERS

America's first farmers domesticated a number of crops. These crops were well suited to the land on which they lived.

Mesoamerica

Some of the earliest American farmers lived in the central part of what is now Mexico. Beginning in 8000–7000 B.C. they began to plant and harvest bottle gourds and pumpkins.

Three to four thousand years later the crops that farmers in the Tehuacán Valley grew included corn, three types of beans, chili peppers, avocados, two kinds of squash, and amaranth (a plant grown for its seeds). Later they began to cultivate sunflowers and then manioc, a root crop first domesticated in the Amazon River Basin. In the centuries before the Spaniards arrived, they became full-time farmers and had begun to grow more varieties of beans and squash as well as tobacco.

The first Europeans to see and taste the crops the Mesoamerican farmers grew were astonished by the amount and variety of the food that Indians grew. They took seeds and plants to Europe and to their Asian and African colonies.

South America

At about the same time that ancient people living in what is now Mexico domesticated crops, American Indians living in what is now the central part of the Andes in Peru discovered how to farm too. Their efforts focused on quinoa and tubers. Potatoes are the best-known tubers.

These farmers began planting and harvesting potatoes about 10,000 years ago. They developed many different varieties of potatoes and grew sweet potatoes as well. They also domesticated three other tubers: oca, mashua, and ullucu. These plants are still eaten by the people of the Andes, but Europeans did not adopt them.

▲▽▲▽▲▽▲▽▲▽▲▽▲▽▲▽▲▽▲▽▲▽▲▽▲

MODERN USES FOR ANCIENT CROPS

Today scientists concerned about world hunger are taking a second look at American Indian crops that are not widely grown or known throughout the world. Some think that plants such as oca, mashua, and ullucu could help solve the hunger problem if farmers around the globe began to grow them. The contributions of American Indian farmers to the world's people may be beginning anew as these ancient crops are used for food.

▽▲▽▲▽▲▽▲▽▲▽▲▽▲▽▲▽▲▽▲▽▲▽▲▽

In addition to domesticating plants for food, the people of the Andes also began herding and domesticating llama as a source of food. They started raising *cuy,* or guinea pigs, for meat as well.

South American farmers who lived in the Amazon River Basin domesticated manioc, or cassava. This root crop provides maximum food energy with very little labor on the part of farmers.

North America

Indians living in the Northeast and Southeast of what is now the United States independently began cultivating goosefoot, marsh elder or sumpweed, and sunflowers. They also domesticated erect knotweed, little barley, and maygrass—all seed-producing grasses.

These crops, except for sunflowers, are relatively unknown to most people today. They once provided a balanced diet for American Indian people. Because these plants produced many seeds, five people could harvest a 200-square-foot field, planted equally with marsh elder, or sumpweed, and chenopod in a

▲▽▲▽▲▽▲▽▲▽▲▽▲▽▲▽▲▽▲▽▲▽▲▽▲

BOTTLE GOURDS

Bottle gourds have tough skins and very little flesh. The gourds range from light to dark green in color. From four to 40 inches long, they grow on climbing vines. They are sturdy, fast-growing plants. American Indians dried bottle gourds and used them for eating and cooking utensils, canteens, rattles and whistles. Eastern Woodland Indians sometimes hung gourds on poles in their fields to serve as homes for insect-eating birds.

▽▲▽▲▽▲▽▲▽▲▽▲▽▲▽▲▽▲▽▲▽▲▽▲▽

little more than a week. A field this size provided half the food needed by 10 people for six months. By about 4,000 years ago American Indians living in the river valleys of what are now Tennessee, Arkansas, Illinois, Kentucky, Ohio, Missouri, and Alabama had also domesticated squash and bottle gourds.

Corn seeds were first introduced to these farmers in about A.D. 200, but corn did not become a major crop for them until about A.D. 800.

HOW THE FIRST FARMERS GREW CROPS

Before they could harvest crops, American Indian farmers needed to clear the land, till the soil, and plant seeds.

Clearing the Land

Indian farmers chose land where few large trees grew. Next they cut down the small trees and brush with stone axes, evenly spreading them across the earth that was to become a field. This method of clearing land is called milpa, swidden, or slash-and-burn agriculture. It is still practiced by indigenous farmers in parts of Mexico and South America.

American Indians discovered that if they cut a strip of bark from around the trunk of larger trees, those trees would die within one to three years. Removing the bark from around the tree prevented the food that the tree made in its leaves from reaching the roots. These Indians usually cleared land in the spring because this was easiest and most effective time to remove the tree bark.

Once the large trees had died, Indian farmers could more easily cut them down or burn them where they stood. This method of controlling trees is called tree girdling. Today it is still used by organic farmers and landscapers, who do not want to use chemicals to remove trees from their land.

▲▽▲▽▲▽▲▽▲▽▲▽▲▽▲▽▲▽▲▽▲▽▲▽▲▽▲▽▲

MILPA TODAY

Today milpa is still practiced in Mesoamerica and in South America's Amazon River Basin, but this is changing. Population growth and the pressure to make more money have forced Native farmers to shorten fallow (nongrowing) periods and sometimes abandon them. Big multinational businesses are urging indigenous farmers to clear huge tracts of land in order to raise cattle. Many scientists are concerned that this is disturbing the delicate ecological balance of the rain forest.

▽▲▽▲▽▲▽▲▽▲▽▲▽▲▽▲▽▲▽▲▽▲▽▲▽▲▽▲▽

When the branches and brush that the farmers cleared had dried, they set fire to them. The ashes that remained after the fire reduced soil acidity. Burning also added magnesium, calcium, potash, and phosphorus to the soil. Proper balance of these minerals is important to plant growth. In addition, burning increased nitrogen in the soil. Nitrogen is necessary to grow healthy bean plants. Rather than planting the newly cleared plots of land right away, most farmers waited a year or two before growing crops on them.

American Indians understood that the nutrients in the earth were used up by constant planting, so after two or three seasons of growing crops on one field, they cleared new fields. In the Northeast, Huron farmers' fields typically yielded about 25 to 30 bushels of corn an acre. When yields dropped to a third of that, they cleared new plots. Every 10 to 12 years they relocated their villages. In Mesoamerica, Maya farmers let their fields lie unused from 15 to 40 years before using them again.

Europeans, eager to use the fields that the Indians had cleared, drove them from their farms, permanently relocating them to land that in many cases was unsuitable for farming.

Tilling the Soil

After they had cleared their plots (small fields), American Indian farmers used digging sticks or foot plows to loosen the soil and break it into fine pieces for planting. Archaeologists believe that the people who lived in what is now Peru were the first to use foot plows to till the soil about 10,000 years ago.

Using foot plows, Native farmers were able to plant enough crops to feed people who lived in some of the most populous cities in the world. Tenochtitlán, the capital of the Aztec Empire, had more inhabitants than Paris did at the time when the Spanish conquistador Hernán Cortés first saw it in 1519. In the Andes Mountains, ancient

Andean farmers used a foot plow to plant potatoes in this drawing by Indian artist Felipe Guamán Poma de Ayala published in 1615. Foot plows were used throughout the Americas. (Nueva corónica y buen gobierno)

Indian farmers made 1.5 million acres of fields. Their small plots of land added up to a great deal of farming.

Farmers of the Americas did not use wedge-shaped plows that were pulled by draft animals until after contact with Europeans. Foot plows were more suited to their environment since no animals native to the Americans could easily be trained to pull such a plow. America's first farmers invented very efficient ways to raise food on the land that they had cleared. These methods were very different from those in many other parts of the world, where crops were planted in rows.

Planting the Crops

Rather than planting seeds in rows, American Indian farmers grew several types of plants together in small plots. Indians either planted several types of plants in the same small hill or grouped them together in flat fields. Planting several types of crops together increased the amount of food a farmer could grow in a small plot. It also helped the plants to grow because they helped each other. This is now known as "companion planting."

Northeast farmers often planted corn, beans, and squash in the same hill. Corn stalks provided a place for the bean runners to climb. Bacteria that grew on the roots of the bean plants stored nitrogen from the air, releasing some of it to the soil. Corn, like beans, needs large amounts of nitrogen in order to prosper.

The tall corn stalks shaded the squash plants that covered the ground. In turn, the broad, low leaves of the squash plants kept the ground from drying out too quickly. Because

By the time Europeans arrived, farmers of the Northeast were expert farmers. This engraving of the village of Secotan in what is now Virginia was made by Theodore De Bry between 1590 and 1598. *(Library of Congress, Prints and Photographs Division [LC-USZ62-52444])*

▲▽▲▽▲▽▲▽▲▽▲▽▲▽▲▽▲▽▲▽▲▽▲▽▲

FOOT PLOWS

American Indian farmers made a foot plow from a wooden pole about six feet long with a two-inch diameter. They sharpened the end that was used to till the soil to a point. Then they heated the pole over a fire to harden it. Finally they attached a little platform for a footrest about 12 inches from the bottom of the plow. Farmers broke the soil for planting by stepping on the footrest.

▽▲▽▲▽▲▽▲▽▲▽▲▽▲▽▲▽▲▽▲▽▲▽▲▽

squash plants fought with weeds for space, sunlight, and nourishment from the soil, American Indian farmers had less weeding to do. Companion planting also helped control insects. Beans and squash attract insects that eat the pests that target and destroy corn.

Native farmers of the desert Southwest did not do much companion planting. Instead they developed bush beans that did not climb by sending out runners and so did not need corn stalks to support them. Plants in the desert need to be spaced far enough apart so that they do not compete for moisture. Desert farmers of the Southwest found another way to control insects as well. They kept squash bugs from destroying their plants by sprinkling ashes on the leaves.

▲▽▲▽▲▽▲▽▲▽▲▽▲▽▲▽▲▽▲▽▲▽▲▽▲

THE THREE SISTERS

People of some tribes called corn, beans, and squash the three sisters. Not only did these three food plants help each other to grow when they were planted together, they provided excellent nutrition. Together the amino acids in corn and beans provide a complete protein, something neither food does on its own. The vitamins in squash, including beta-carotene and vitamin C, work together with those provided by the other sister vegetables.

▽▲▽▲▽▲▽▲▽▲▽▲▽▲▽▲▽▲▽▲▽▲▽▲▽

Today Maya farmers in Mesoamerica continue to use companion planting as their ancestors did. Sometimes they grow as many as 60 to 80 kinds of crops in one plot. Even tiny plots contain a dozen or more types of plants.

5

Agriculture Changes and Grows

As time passed, Indian farmers of the Americas grew many crops that flourished in a number of climates. One of the ways they did this was by saving seeds from plants that had traits they wanted. If they wanted to grow taller corn, they saved kernels from their tallest corn plants. They then planted only these seeds. When the seeds matured, they again saved kernels from the tallest plants in this new crop. After they had selected and saved seeds from many generations of corn plants, these farmers had developed a new, taller variety of corn. This practice is called seed selection.

Ancient farmers selected seeds from plants that produced larger or more seeds or fruits than other plants did. They selected seeds from plants that could resist disease. They also saved seeds from plants that needed less moisture than other plants and from those that required a shorter growing season. American Indians used seed selection to make chili peppers taste hotter and corn taste sweeter. Using seed selection, Indian farmers from North America to South America changed the genetic make-up of the crops they planted. They created thousands of varieties of crops.

SAVING SEEDS TO CREATE CORN

About 7,000 years ago farmers of Mesoamerica began selecting seeds from a wild grass plant called teosinite (*Zea mexicana*). Teosinite had many stalks and only a few seeds. Slowly, after thousands of years, American Indian farmers had created maize (*Zea mays*), or corn. Corn is a crop that does not grow in the wild and can only survive if it is planted and tended by human beings.

The first corn that American Indians grew had small ears that contained only six to nine kernels. By about 2,000 years ago, Indian farmers were expert corn breeders, producing plants with single stalks and larger ears. The first corn they developed was the type called popcorn today.

The farmers planted different types of corn side by side so that they would cross-pollinate. In this way they created even more varieties of corn. By the time Columbus landed in the Americas in 1492, Indians had created more than 700 varieties of corn through seed selection and crossbreeding. A number of these varieties, including popcorn, are still grown and eaten today.

These corncobs from the Tehuacán Valley excavation in central Mexico show how corn developed from 5000 B.C. to A.D. 1500. Ancient Indian farmers used seed selection to develop corn. *(Robert S. Peabody Museum of Archaeology, Phillips Academy, Andover, Massachusetts)*

DISCOVERING NEW FARMING METHODS

As they created new types of crops, American Indian farmers also discovered new and better ways to grow them. They invented irrigation, terraced farming, and fertilizer independently from people in other parts of the world. Indian farmers were the only people in the world to use double cropping, or multiple cropping, as a form of food insurance.

Controlling the Water Supply with Irrigation

When American Indians first began farming, they planted their fields in river valleys or near streams. Water that flooded the banks of the rivers provided moisture for crops and added nutrients to the soil. In order to farm on these floodplains American Indians needed to know a great deal about runoff and stream flow. If the crops received too little water they would not grow. If they received too much water, they would wash away or rot.

Indian farmers later discovered how to better control the amount of water they provided for their crops by building irrigation canals. These canals channeled water to the fields they had planted. This meant they could farm in other places besides floodplains. The Olmec of Mesoamerica built some of the earliest canals a little more than 4,000 years ago.

▲▼▲▼▲▼▲▼▲▼▲▼▲▼▲▼▲▼▲▼▲▼▲▼▲▼▲

SAVING ANCIENT CROPS

American Indian farmers worked to develop many more crops than did people in other parts of the world. Unlike ancient Indian farmers, modern farmers grow huge amounts of only a few types of plants. Although many varieties of Indian crops are grown today, many are not. The genes from these plant varieties that Indian farmers created are disappearing. Some scientists believe that the world's food supply may be in danger because of this.

The organization Native Seeds/SEARCH makes sure that these seeds do not become extinct. They have saved seeds from more than 350 plants first grown by American Indian farmers of the desert Southwest. The Eastern Native Seed Conservancy preserves seeds from plants once grown by Indian farmers of the Northeast. These seeds include sweet corn, beans, and pumpkins.

▼▲▼▲▼▲▼▲▼▲▼▲▼▲▼▲▼▲▼▲▼▲▼▲▼▲▼

Saving Soil with Terraces

Fields built like stair steps into the sides of hills or mountains are called terraces. Indian farmers of the Americas discovered that if they built walled terraces this would keep rainwater from washing soil down the slope. When water washes topsoil from the land, this is called erosion. Slowing the flow of water allowed it to sink into the soil, so it was also an effective form of irrigation. Terraced fields allowed Indian people to grow crops on land that had once been unsuitable for farming.

Enriching the Soil with Fertilizer

Natural fertilizer is organic matter that adds nutrients to the soil so that it produces healthy plants with high yield. Clearing land by cutting brush and burning it added some nutrients to the soil. Native farmers of the Americas also began experimenting to find other fertilizers. Fields that had been fertilized could be used longer before new fields needed to be cleared. Improving the soil also allowed Indian farmers to plant crops in areas with poor soil for farming.

Multiple Cropping to Ensure the Food Supply

Indian farmers planted each of their crops two or more times during the growing season. This gave them a steady supply of fresh food. Planting more than once was a way to ensure that bad weather, plant disease, or insects would not destroy the farmers' entire crop.

AGRICULTURE EXPANDS

With these discoveries, farming spread from river valleys and areas with good rainfall and rich soil where it had first begun. People in the dry, hot desert of the North American Southwest began farming. Indian farmers traveled up the Missouri River valley and began to farm the northern Great Plains where growing seasons are very short. Farmers in the Northeast and Southeast planted enough crops to feed large villages. In the meantime, farmers in Mesoamerica and the Andes of South America started producing abundant food to support more and more people. They built huge cities and created the Maya, Aztec, and Inca empires.

Farming in the Southwest

The Indian farmers who lived in the desert of what is now Arizona began growing corn about 3,500 years ago. A thousand years later they had become expert farmers and had created plants adapted to the desert. One of these plants was a bush bean that withstood the desert climate and needed little water.

The Hohokam farmers, who grew corn, beans, squash, cotton, and tobacco, coped with the dry climate by building irrigation canals along the Salt and Gila River Valleys. After about 500 years of working with stone hoes and wooden digging sticks and rakes, the Hohokam had built more than 150 miles of canals that were 10 feet deep. Farmers used brush and sand to divert river water into the canals. Gravity carried the water to vegetable gardens as far as 30 miles from the rivers. They plastered the canals to keep the water from seeping into the dry ground. The canals served many villages and towns.

In the late 1880s white settlers in the Salt River Valley began using the ancient irrigation system. Today the city of Phoenix, Arizona, continues to use many of the canals that the Hohokam built.

The Anasazi people, who lived in the desert Southwest, also found ways to make sure their fields had enough water. They made

From May to September the desert where the Hohokam lived is hot—from 100°F to 120°F. Only about six to eight inches of rain falls in a year. Most of this rain comes during July and August.

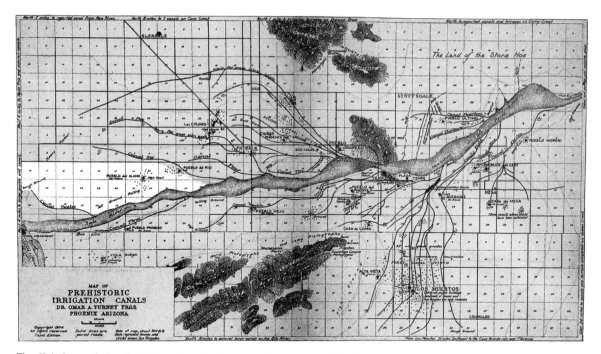

The Hohokam of the North American Southwest built a system of irrigation canals on the land that would later become Phoenix, Arizona. Non-Indian farmers later also used these canals. *(Arizona State Museum, University of Arizona)*

lines of rocks on thousands of acres of sloping land. These terraces slowed the water runoff and held the soil in place.

Anasazi farmers also built small dams at the top of the streams that developed after storms. In Mesa Verde, a large Anasazi settlement in the southwest of what is now Colorado, archaeologists discovered hundreds of such dams after a 1996 fire. In addition the Anasazi built reservoirs to store water and ditches and lined stones so water could flow to their fields.

Farming on the Great Plains

The Mandan, Hidatsa, and Arikira carried their farming traditions with them up the Missouri River to what is now North Dakota. They used seed selection to develop the great northern bean, which was especially suited to short growing seasons. This variety of bean is still grown by farmers today.

Indian farmers of the plains found other ways to meet the challenges of their climate. They started squash seeds inside their homes in spring to give them a head start. First they covered a piece of buffalo hide with wet grass and leaves. Then they sprinkled it with squash seeds. Finally they folded it into a bundle and hung it on a pole beside the fire in their earth lodge homes. When the seeds had sprouted and the earth was warm, they planted the seedlings in the ground.

Once their fields had been planted and the crops had begun to mature, these farmers built platforms in the middle of their fields. Girls and women took turns sitting on the platforms to keep birds from eating the crops.

Farming in the Northeast and Southeast

Like farmers of the Great Plains, northeastern farmers developed varieties of crops that would mature quickly. Indian people from the lower part of what is now Canada to what is now Florida grew corn, pumpkins, squash, and sunflowers, as well as other plants that are not as well known today.

Huron women transplanted tender young squash plants as the Hidatsa did. They started their squash seeds in bark trays that they had filled with a potting soil made of moistened, powdered wood. They kept these trays beside their cooking fires, planting the squash after the danger of frost was gone. Colonists in New England who saw Huron women transplanting seedlings began doing the same in their own gardens. Transplanting is a common practice among gardeners today.

Indian farmers of the Northeast are best known for using fish as fertilizer. Squanto, a Patuxet, shared his knowledge of farming with the Pilgrims, who established the Massachusetts Bay Colony in 1620.

▲▽▲▽▲▽▲▽▲▽▲▽▲▽▲▽▲▽▲▽▲▽▲▽▲▽▲

TRADING CORN

By the late 1600s Indians near Lake Erie and Lake Ontario grew corn to feed their own people and to trade with other tribes. Their fields were so large that a party of early French explorers became lost in them when walking from village to village.

▼▲▼▲▼▲▼▲▼▲▼▲▼▲▼▲▼▲▼▲▼▲▼▲▼▲▼

▽▲▽▲▽▲▽▲▽▲▽▲▽▲▽▲▽▲▽▲▽▲▽▲▽▲▽▲▽▲▽▲▽▲

FISH AS FERTILIZER

The Indian people did not eat menhaden, the fish Squanto used for fertilizer. The names they gave them, *munnoquo-hatean* or *munnawhatteauq*, meant "that which enriches the soil." The colonists quickly adopted the use of fish fertilizer. Fish meal is still used for fertilizer today.

▽▲▽▲▽▲▽▲▽▲▽▲▽▲▽▲▽▲▽▲▽▲▽▲▽▲▽▲▽▲▽▲▽▲

Recently returned from captivity in Europe, he had learned to speak English. In the spring of 1621 he taught the Pilgrims to plant corn, a grain they had never seen before, and to fertilize it with fish.

American Indians of the Northeast and Southeast also planted herbs they used as medicines. Early European observers wrote about seeing these herb gardens growing near abandoned Indian villages.

Farming in Mesoamerica

Maya farmers invented a very effective way to feed a large number of people. In addition to farming regular plots, they built artificial islands in swamplands and lakes. These islands, called *chinampas*, were ideal places to grow crops.

Later, the Aztec in the Valley of Mexico became expert chinampas farmers. As more people began living in the city of Tenochtitlán, which was on a lakeshore, farmers made more plots in order to grow enough food for them. (This is the site of what would become Mexico City.) By the 1500s, these islands nearly covered two large lakes. Eventually farmers recovered more than 46 square miles of swamps. They were able to grow enough food to feed the 100,000 to 250,000 people who lived in the nearby city.

▽▲▽▲▽▲▽▲▽▲▽▲▽▲▽▲▽▲▽▲▽▲▽▲▽▲▽▲

SALT WATER TO FRESH

Aztec engineers changed Lake Texcoco, a large saltwater lake, into a freshwater lake. They did so by building a network of gated dikes and raised water channels from a nearby freshwater spring to the lake. Then they built many chinampas on Lake Texcoco.

▽▲▽▲▽▲▽▲▽▲▽▲▽▲▽▲▽▲▽▲▽▲▽▲▽▲▽▲

To build chinampas, the Aztec dug long, straight canals at the edges of lakes or through swamps to drain them of much water. Next they piled soil between these large ditches to form raised beds. Finally they allowed the canals between the islands to fill with water. The island gardens were four or five feet above the waterline so that the roots of crops were not waterlogged. Farmers planted trees there so that their roots would help hold the earth in place.

Soil that eroded from the plots fell into the canals, where it nourished water plants. Each season, before planting crops, the farmers harvested the water plants and piled them on the raised beds to fertilize the soil. They also collected the soil that had washed into the canals and replaced it on the beds. The canals attracted fish, and the islands attracted birds. Both could be eaten.

Chinampas farmers built their homes on raised beds in the middle of the swamps and traveled to their fields in canoes. Often they started seeds on long rafts piled with earth. They towed these behind their canoes.

In addition to inventing raised-bed agriculture, ancient Mesoamerican farmers created orchards where they grew cashews as well as guava, papaya, avocado, sapodilla, and sapote trees. Maya and Aztec people also surrounded their homes with fruit trees. When the Spaniards colonized the Yucatán peninsula, they forced the Maya to move near the towns they had built around churches. To make them leave, the Spaniards burned their old towns and cut down the fruit trees.

> Many of today's gardeners create raised beds in order to save water and to grow vegetables in a small area.

BOTANICAL GARDENS

The Aztec planted botanical gardens with huge collections of plants native to the area and those imported from the tropical coast hundreds of miles distant. These gardens were for the amusement and education of those who visited them. Spanish historian Cervantes de Salazar described the gardens of the Emperor Montezuma (Moctezuma) as containing "medicinal and aromatic herbs," flowers, and trees with fragrant blossoms.

Mesoamerican farmers developed a number of agricultural techniques that enabled them to feed the thousands of people who lived in urban areas. This picture of Aztec farmers cultivating their fields was made in about 1525. *(Library of Congress, Prints and Photographs Division [LC-USZ62-124461])*

Farming in South America

Ancient farmers of the Andes were experts at terraced farming. They grew beans, potatoes, and a seed crop called quinoa on the steep slopes of mountain valleys. They started by using rocks to contain the soil of their flat plots. Later they carved giant stone blocks. By the time of the Inca Empire, 1,000 years later, they had created hundreds of acres of terraces. The Inca watered many of their terraced fields from reservoirs and from streams that they diverted to the fields using stone channels. Peruvian farmers still use many of these plots today.

High in the Andes at Machu Picchu, the Inca planted what seem to be experimental plots. They established these plots at a number of altitudes and in places that received various amounts of sunlight and shade. This practice allowed them to grow very high yields of potatoes and corn and to develop a number of varieties that were suited to different soils and climates.

Indian farmers of the Andes fertilized their crops with llama dung and anchovy heads. They also gathered guano (bird droppings) from islands off the seacoast to enrich the soil. Over the centuries, birds had left mountains of these droppings on the islands.

When the Spaniards arrived, they began selling the guano. By the 1700s, they were shipping it throughout the world. In the mid-1800s guano fertilizer from Peru was sold in the United States and in Europe.

▲▽▲▽▲▽▲▽▲▽▲▽▲▽▲▽▲▽▲▽▲▽▲▽▲▽▲▽▲▽▲

GUANO

The Inca, whose empire was established in about A.D. 1000, divided the guano deposits into districts. They marked different areas and allotted them to specific groups of farmers. The farmers hauled guano from the deposits on inflated rafts made of sealskin.

▼▲▼▲▼▲▼▲▼▲▼▲▼▲▼▲▼▲▼▲▼▲▼▲▼▲▼▲▼▲▼

Farmers in the tropical regions of South America cultivated as many as 140 types of crops. Many of these were nuts and fruits. Today many anthropologists believe that as much as 12 percent of the Amazon forest was either directly or indirectly created by ancient farmers. They introduced new plants to the forest and changed the places where wild plants grew.

Much of the soil in the Amazon Basin of what is now Brazil does not contain the proper nutrients to support farming. Tropical forests receive a great deal of rain that washes these nutrients from the soil. Other areas of the rain forest contain *terra preta* (dark earth), a very

Indian farmers of the Andes created hundreds of acres of terraced fields near Cuzco, the Inca capital. *(Neg. No. 334768; Photo: Shippee-Johnson, Courtesy Department of Library Services, American Museum of Natural History)*

rich, black soil. It contains special bacteria that quickly break down organic matter such as dead plants into nutrients that growing plants can use.

American Indian farmers in the Amazon Basin improved the quality of the poor soil by mixing *terra preta* with it. After a short time, the bacteria changed the poor soil into nutrient-rich soil. Many groups of people in the Amazon Basin did this. Over a long period of time they changed the soil composition in large areas so that they could grow food.

TIME LINE	
1700 B.C.	The Olmec of Mesoamerica begin to use irrigation.
1500 B.C.	The Maya begin building chinampas, artificial islands, where they grow their crops.
1500 B.C.	Indian farmers of the Southwest start growing corn.
600 B.C.	Hohokam farmers begin building irrigation canals.
300 B.C.	Farmers of the Andes build mountainside terraces using huge limestone blocks.
A.D. 1	Mesoamerican farmers have become expert corn growers using seed selection.
A.D. 200	American Indians bring corn seed to the Northeast.
A.D. 800	Corn becomes a major crop for farmers of the Northeast.
A.D. 1000–A.D. 1200	Anasazi farmers build dikes and small dams to water their fields.
A.D. 1500	Mesoamerican farmers feed from 100,000 to 250,000 people with the food they grow on chinampas.

6

Major American Indian Food Crops

The food crops that were most important for American Indian farmers were those that contained high nutritional value. How much work was needed to grow a crop also determined how much of it American Indian farmers grew. Although Indian people raised some crops that required a great deal of time and effort, these foods tended to make up a smaller part of their diet.

THREE SISTERS: UNIVERSAL CROPS

Indian people in North, Meso-, and South America raised the "three sisters"—corn, beans, and squash. These three food crops had a central place in their diets.

Corn

Corn (*Zea mays*) is high in starch, a substance that the human body changes to sugar in order to provide fuel for activity. In addition to

THE MANY NAMES OF CORN

Tribes throughout North and Central America had many names for corn. Many of these names meant "our mother" or "our life." The Spanish called it "maize" after the Taino word *mahis*, which means "source of life." The British, who call grain *corn*, used that name, which is still used in the United States.

Corn was a major crop for Indian farmers throughout the Americas, who developed it from a wild grass. *(PhotoDisc)*

B vitamins, magnesium, potassium, and vitamin C, it is high in fiber.

Mesoamerican Indians used corn in many ways. They ate ripe corn as a fresh vegetable and ground dry corn kernels into flour and meal. They also heated corn to pop it. Because the leaves and stalks of corn plant are sweet, the Maya used them as the first "chewing gum." By the 1400s corn made up 80 percent of the Maya diet.

Farmers of the Northeast grew corn to eat and to trade with other tribes. The Huron raised enough corn to store a two-to-four-year surplus. Northeast Indians found many uses for the corn plant besides food. They used husks to make moccasins, mats, and baskets. They even stored medicine in hollowed stalks.

The Spaniards took corn to their colonies in the Philippines, Africa, and Asia. They also carried it to Europe, where it became popular in the Mediterranean. For many years northern Europeans used corn primarily as animal food.

Today corn is one of the most important crops grown in the world. It is eaten fresh or made into meal, coarse flour that is used in baked goods, cereals, and snack chips. Corn is also used for oil and sweetener. Each year each person in the United States eats more than 28 pounds of corn products such as cornmeal, corn flour, and hominy. They also eat almost 90 pounds of corn sweeteners every year.

This American Indian crop has more than 3,500 different uses. Scientists make 100 percent biodegradable plastics from corn, which might help solve the problem of overflowing landfills. A superabsorbent corn-

Corn became an important part of the diet of American people. This poster made in 1918, during World War I, urges people to eat more of it in order to be patriotic. *(Lloyd Harrison, artist/Library of Congress, Prints and Photographs Division [LC-USZC4-10124])*

starch that soaks up 300 times its weight in water is used in some disposable diapers and automobile fuel filters. Corn is also used to deice roads. Ethanol, an alcohol made from corn, is blended with gasoline to help reduce air pollution.

Beans

Beans are legumes, plants with root nodules that contain bacteria. These bacteria help them obtain nitrogen from the soil. Bean plants bear pods that contain seeds. Dry beans that have been allowed to ripen on the vine contain 20 to 25 percent protein and very little fat. They are high in fiber, folic acid, B vitamins, and potassium.

Indians of Mesoamerica and South America developed green beans about 7,500 years ago. Using seed selection, they created black beans, lima beans, navy beans, and pinto beans, to name just a few. Later the Hohokam people of the Southwest grew kidney beans and jack beans. Native farmers of the Ohio Valley grew beans, as did farmers in parts of the Northeast. Great Plains farmers developed great northern beans. This variety, which has a short growing season, is planted extensively today.

The explorer Hernán Cortés sent beans to King Charles I of Spain. Before Europeans grew these beans, they raised only fava beans and lentils. Beans never became popular in Europe, but they were important in European colonists' diets. Today each person in the United States eats about 7.5 pounds of dry beans every year.

Two of Christopher Columbus's men brought him samples of flour made from corn. This was the first corn Europeans had eaten. After Columbus tried it, he wrote in his journal that it was "well tasted."

▲▼▲▼▲▼▲▼▲▼▲▼▲▼▲▼▲▼▲▼▲▼▲▼▲▼▲▼▲▼▲▼

GREEN BEANS

Green beans are picked and cooked before they are ripe while the pods are still soft. The green part of the bean is its pod. "Green" beans can also be purple or yellow. Other names for green beans are garden beans, string beans, pole beans, snap beans, and haricots.

▼▲▼▲▼▲▼▲▼▲▼▲▼▲▼▲▼▲▼▲▼▲▼▲▼▲▼▲▼▲▼▲▼

Squash

Squash is a fleshy fruit-producing plant. It contains vitamins C and E and beta-carotene, a substance that the body converts to vitamin A. Indian farmers developed many varieties. These included

Pumpkins are only one of many varieties of squash. American Indians dried the seeds and ate them for a high-energy snack. *(PhotoDisc)*

The word *squash* comes from a Narragansett word, *askutasquash*. It means "a green thing that is eaten raw."

zucchini, pumpkins, gourds, and acorn and yellow squash. They also developed butternut and hubbard squash.

Squash was so important to southwestern tribes that the squash blossom came to be a symbol of fertility for the Hopi. It is a common design in turquoise and silver jewelry made by southwestern Native artisans today.

Spanish and French explorers thought that American Indian squash and pumpkin fields were melon patches at first. Spaniards carried seeds to Spain in the 1500s. Two hundred years later Italian gardeners were growing zucchini. Other Europeans ground squash seeds to make candy instead of eating squash as a vegetable.

NORTH AMERICAN CROPS

In addition to the three sisters, sunflowers were an important crop for Indian farmers of the Southwest, Northeast, and Great Plains.

Sunflowers

Sunflowers produce large yellow flowers on stems that grow more than five feet tall. The large sunflower "bloom" is really 1,000 to 2,000 tiny flowers. Each produces a seed encased in a thin shell. One ounce of sunflower seeds contains 160 calories, most of them in the form of unsaturated fats. This makes them a high-energy food. They also contain vitamin E, foliate, zinc, and fiber. American Indians of the Southwest were the first to grow them. Later American Indians of the Northeast raised them as well.

American Indians ate sunflower seeds as a snack. They also removed the oil from the seeds by boiling them in water and skimming it from the surface. They used this oil as hairdressing and skin lotion. Hidatsa farmers of the Great Plains planted sunflowers around fields containing other crops in order to form a living fence.

The Spaniards took sunflower seeds to Europe, where they were grown as ornamentals. About 300 years later Russian people began growing them for food. Today farmers in the United States grow sunflower seeds to make cooking oil. Sunflowers are also used for bird-

Sunflowers were a source of oil for American Indians. The Hidatsa of the Plains ground them and shaped them into balls to eat as trail food. *(PhotoDisc)*

seed and cattle feed. Because sunflower oil has only slightly lower energy content than diesel fuel, some scientists believe it could become a diesel fuel substitute.

MESOAMERICAN CROPS

Amaranth and chili peppers were an important part of Mesoamerican Indians' diet in addition to corn, beans, and squash.

Amaranth

Amaranth is a cereal plant, native to the Americas, that needs little moisture. It produces seeds that are 13 to 18 percent higher in protein than other cereal grains. The seeds contain as much of the amino acid lysine as milk and twice the lysine of wheat. Amaranth also contains high levels of calcium, vitamin E, and B vitamins. These nutritious seeds were one of the main foods of the Maya and Aztec peoples.

Today the seeds that the Aztec called *huahtli* are again eaten. Amaranth is an important part of the diet for people living in India, China, Pakistan, Tibet, and Nepal. Amaranth is sold as a health food in the United States.

▲▽▲▽▲▽▲▽▲▽▲▽▲▽▲▽▲▽▲▽▲▽▲▽▲▽▲▽▲

AN ILLEGAL PLANT

The first European to describe amaranth saw Indian people eating amaranth tamales during religious ceremonies. He thought this was a mockery of Catholic communion. Soon afterward, the Spaniards outlawed amaranth cultivation, sale, and consumption under penalty of death in an effort to stop Aztec religious practices.

▽▲▽▲▽▲▽▲▽▲▽▲▽▲▽▲▽▲▽▲▽▲▽▲▽▲▽▲▽

Chili Peppers

Chili peppers are related to potatoes, tomatoes, and tobacco, which are also native to the Americas. Chilies contain twice the vitamin C of citrus fruits. They are one of the first plants that American Indians domesticated about 9,000 years ago. Maya and Aztec farmers developed dozens of chili varieties. Today, after salt, chili is the most used seasoning in the world.

▲▽▲▽▲▽▲▽▲▽▲▽▲▽▲▽▲▽▲▽▲▽▲▽▲▽▲▽▲▽▲▽▲

A PASSION FOR CHILIES

Chili is an Aztec word. According to some accounts, the Aztec ate chilies for breakfast, lunch, and dinner. They spiced chocolate drinks with them, used them as medicine, and paid taxes with them.

▽▲▽▲▽▲▽▲▽▲▽▲▽▲▽▲▽▲▽▲▽▲▽▲▽▲▽▲▽▲▽▲▽

Chili peppers get their flavor from capsaicin, a substance in the seeds and membranes. A dominant gene—one that sweet peppers lack—determines the amount of capsaicin in a pepper. Through seed selection, Indian farmers controlled the amount of capsaicin in the peppers they raised. These farmers knew that poor soil or hot temperatures cause chili peppers to make more capsaicin. They used these factors to turn up the heat in their peppers. Although Indians grew both hot and sweet peppers, they preferred chilies.

Columbus brought chilies to Spain in 1493. One hundred years later the chili trade was booming. In addition to being eaten, today capsicum from chili peppers is used to repel rodents and insects. It is the basis for pepper spray carried as a self-defense device. Chili chemicals are used for dyes in cosmetics, lunch meats, and salad dressing. Farmers feed chickens red chilies to make their egg yolks darker, and zookeepers feed it to flamingos to make their feathers more brilliant.

SOUTH AMERICAN CROPS

The most significant crops that the Indian farmers of South America grew to feed their people were potatoes, manioc, quinoa, and sweet potatoes.

Potatoes

Potatoes are a tuber crop. Because potatoes are easily grown in a number of climates and are high

American Indians of the Southwest continue to grow chili peppers today. The man in this picture is hanging chilies that have been strung in order to dry them in the sun. It was taken at Isleta Pueblo in 1940. *(Library of Congress, Prints and Photographs Division [LC-USF33-012932-M3])*

▲▽▲▽▲▽▲▽▲▽▲▽▲▽▲▽▲▽▲▽▲▽▲▽▲▽▲▽▲▽▲▽▲

POTATOES

In 1531, when Spanish conquistador Francisco Pizarro landed in what is now Peru, the indigenous Andean people had developed about 3,000 types of potatoes and had also invented a method to freeze-dry them for storage.

▽▲▽▲▽▲▽▲▽▲▽▲▽▲▽▲▽▲▽▲▽▲▽▲▽▲▽▲▽▲▽▲▽

in both vitamin C and starch, they were an efficient way of meeting dietary needs for a number of people.

Indians of the Andes were the first to domesticate potatoes. The earliest potato, found in an archaeological site in central Peru has been dated to about 10,000 years ago. Nine thousand years later, Indian farmers were growing not only white potatoes but red, yellow, black, blue, green, and brown ones as well. They bred potatoes of varying sizes and shapes that would do well under many growing conditions.

The Inca, who called potatoes *papas*, ate boiled potatoes as a vegetable and also made a kind of unleavened potato bread from flour that had been ground from freeze-dried potatoes. They also added this potato flour to soups and stew and made a gruel, or porridge, from it.

Europeans did not care for potatoes when they were first introduced to them. Some people believed they caused diseases. Others considered the potato "the devil's plant" and thought eating it was a sin. Despite this, the Spanish adopted potatoes as standard fare aboard ship. European peasants began growing them as well. A two-and-a-half-acre field of potatoes produced twice as many calories (food energy) as a wheat field of the same size. Potatoes have become one of the most popular vegetables. Today about 250 varieties of potatoes are grown in the United States. Each person in the United States eats an average of 144 pounds of potatoes each year.

Quinoa

Quinoa, pronounced "keenwa," is a seed-bearing plant. Quinoa plants produce thousands of small seeds clustered like plumes at the end of their six-foot-tall stalks. The seeds contain twice the protein of barley, corn, or rice. They are high in the amino acid lysine and fat as well as vitamin E and the B vitamins. South American Indians grew quinoa in the cold, dry climate of the Andes.

The Inca called quinoa *chesiya mama*, which means "the mother of grains." Every year the Inca ruler planted the first quinoa seeds with a golden spade. The Inca fed quinoa to their armies, who ate a mixture of quinoa and fat that they called "war balls."

The Spaniards did not introduce quinoa to Europe. Although they encouraged Indian farmers to substitute European crops, such as wheat and barley, for quinoa, they continued to grow quinoa. Today it continues to be grown in many South American countries. Quinoa seeds, flour, and cereals are sold in health food stores. Saponin from quinoa is used to make detergents, shampoos, beer, photographic chemicals, fire-extinguishing chemicals, and synthetic hormones.

▲▽▲▽▲▽▲▽▲▽▲▽▲▽▲▽▲▽▲▽▲▽▲▽▲▽▲

MORE USES FOR QUINOA

Quinoa seeds are coated with a bitter natural chemical called saponin that discourages birds from eating them. (This is the same chemical some Indian people used to stun fish.) Indians carefully washed quinoa seeds after harvest in order to remove the chemical and make them safe to eat. Andean Indians used the saponin they obtained from washing quinoa as a laundry detergent and as an antiseptic that was used on injuries to the skin.

▽▲▽▲▽▲▽▲▽▲▽▲▽▲▽▲▽▲▽▲▽▲▽▲▽▲▽

Sweet Potatoes

Sweet potatoes are tuberous plants. They produce more pounds of food per acre than any other cultivated plant. High in vitamin C and vitamin A, they contain more sugar and fats than regular potatoes do. Although sweet potatoes are often called yams in North America, the sweet potato is not related to the yam. Neither are sweet potatoes related to regular potatoes. Indian farmers of what are now the Andes were the first to domesticate them about 8,000 to 10,000 years ago. Cultivation spread throughout South America.

After digging batatas from the ground, indigenous people let them cure for several days and then roasted them. This produced a taste that one of the first Europeans to eat sweet potatoes said was as if the vegetable had been dipped into a jar of jam. Spanish conquistadores returned to Spain with sweet potatoes. From there, sweet potatoes traveled to Germany, Belgium, and England.

The Inca called the sweet potato *batata* in Quecha, their language. This word became *potato* in English.

Sweet potatoes are an extremely popular food crop in Asia and in tropical countries today. They are also a popular food in the American South.

Manioc

Manioc or cassava, is a starchy root crop that produces more calories per acre of land than any other crop except for sugarcane. Manioc roots weigh between 10 and 30 pounds. For thousands of years, indigenous people throughout the Amazon Basin, the Circum-Caribbean, and the tropics of South America have cultivated it. Scientists believe many groups of South American Indians independently domesticated manioc.

Some types of manioc could be peeled, cooked, and eaten. Most domesticated manioc, however, contained prussic, or hydrocyanic,

> Because they did not grow well in northern European climates, sweet potatoes were a precious commodity and were even given as gifts as late as 1577.

This early drawing of manioc processing in the Caribbean shows how it was grated on boards that were embedded with stone chips. Grating was an important step in removing toxic juices from the starchy root. (Historie naturelle et morale des îles Antilles de L'Amerique/Stock Montage/The Newberry Library)

acid in small sacs under the root covering. The human digestive system breaks down these chemicals, releasing cyanide into the body. Raw manioc of this type causes poisoning. In order to make manioc edible, American Indians of the tropics invented a way to remove the chemicals.

They peeled raw manioc roots and then shredded them on graters made of stone chips set into wooden boards. Afterward they squeezed the poisonous juice out with presses or hung it in woven fiber tubes. When the juice had dripped out, they washed, roasted, and ground or pounded the grated manioc into meal and baked it.

Indian people who lived in what is now Peru invented another way to make manioc safe to eat. They put the roots in water and allowed them to ferment. Then they placed them in sacks wedged between boards to squeeze the acid out. Afterward they dried pieces of the root, toasted them, and pounded them.

Columbus, the first European to see manioc, wrote in his diary that Indian people planted fields of the tubers. The Portuguese saw Indian farmers growing manioc in what is now Brazil when they arrived there in the early 1500s.

Dried manioc bread keeps for up to three years and resists insects, so the conquistadores ate it on their long sea voyages. The Portuguese carried manioc on their slave ships returning to Africa, where it was quickly adopted. The Spaniards also introduced manioc to the Philippines and eventually to Southeast Asia.

Because of its high food energy and its ability to grow under difficult conditions, manioc changed the course of world history. The

MEAT TENDERIZER AND TAPIOCA

American Indians discovered that if they heated the juice of the manioc, they could remove the poison from it and use it as a meat tenderizer. They also discovered that if they heated the manioc starch that settled from the bottom of the juice, the individual grains popped and clumped together to form tapioca. Today, in addition to serving as a base for the popular pudding, manioc starch is used for laundry starch and sizing. It is also sold as flour.

gift of manioc and the technology to make it edible have provided a staple food for 500 million people worldwide. Most Americans and Europeans today only eat manioc in the form of meat tenderizer, tapioca, and as processed cassava starch used in pudding and fruit pies.

TIME LINE	
8000 B.C.	Indians of the Andes domesticate potatoes.
8000 B.C. to 6000 B.C.	Indians of the Andes domesticate sweet potatoes.
7000 to 5500 B.C.	Mesoamerican farmers domesticate chili peppers.
5500 to 5000 B.C.	Mesoamerican and South American farmers of the Andes independently domesticate beans.
3500 B.C. to 2000 B.C.	American Indian farmers in different areas of South American tropics independently domesticate manioc.
2000 B.C.	Indians of the Andes extensively cultivate potatoes.
3000 B.C.	Indians of the Andes cultivate quinoa.
3400 B.C.	Mesoamerican farmers domesticate wild amaranth.
1500 B.C.	Farmers of the Southwest cultivate beans.
100 B.C. to A.D. 100	Hohokam farmers of the Southwest cultivate kidney beans.

More Foods That American Indians Grew or Raised

7

Indian farmers throughout the Americas cultivated many crops that are still eaten today. Indians of the Americas also raised animals for food.

PLANTS THAT AMERICAN INDIANS GREW

A few of the crops that Mesoamerican farmers grew are avocados, pineapples, and tomatoes. They grew cacao trees to make chocolate and a type of orchid to make vanilla. Ancient farmers of South America domesticated peanuts.

Avocados

Avocados are a green, thick-skinned fruit that grows on trees native to Mesoamerica and the Circum-Caribbean. They are high in vitamins

▲▽▲▽▲▽▲▽▲▽▲▽▲▽▲▽▲▽▲▽▲▽▲▽▲▽▲

COTTON AND TOBACCO

In addition to food crops, American Indian farmers also domesticated other useful plants. Indians of South America domesticated cotton as early as 8,000 years ago. Mesoamerican and Southwest Indian farmers also raised it. Indians throughout the Americas raised tobacco, which they smoked during religious ceremonies.

▽▲▽▲▽▲▽▲▽▲▽▲▽▲▽▲▽▲▽▲▽▲▽▲▽▲▽

A, B$_6$, and C, as well as potassium. American Indians began cultivating them about 4,000 to 5,000 years ago. Later South American farmers grew them. After planting the trees, they had to water and care for them for seven years before they produced fruit. Spanish conquistadores tried taking avocados to Europe, but they spoiled on long ocean voyages. Avocados became popular in the United States in the 1900s.

Cacao

Cacao is a tree native to the Amazon Basin and the tropical lowlands of Mesoamerica. It grows pods that are filled with 20 to 50 whitish seeds. These bitter seeds are used to make chocolate. Maya farmers who grew cacao trees had to protect them from wind and direct sunlight. They also pruned the branches so the trees would grow more pods. To make just one pound of chocolate takes about 400 beans.

The Maya invented chocolate about 2,000 years ago. They opened the pods and scooped out the seeds, which they fermented for several days. This made the beans less bitter and released the chemicals that give chocolate its flavor. Next they roasted the beans and removed their thin shells. Finally they ground them into a paste. They used this paste to make hot and cold drinks. Sometimes they sweetened chocolate with honey or flavored it with chili.

The Toltec, Mixtec, and later the Aztec, who lived in what is now Mexico, ate chocolate too. Since cacao trees did not grow where they lived, they obtained their beans from the Maya through trade and conquest. The Aztec ate solid chocolate, possibly in a form similar to candy bars. They also made chocolate tablets that were dissolved in water to make "instant" chocolate drinks.

In 1519 the Aztec emperor Montezuma (Moctezuma) served Hernán Cortés chocolate. The conquistador returned to Spain with cacao beans and chocolate powder. He believed that chocolate fought tiredness and made the body better able to fight disease. The Spanish priest Father Bernardo Sahagún also considered chocolate to be health food. He wrote that it refreshed people and took away sadness. He cautioned, however, that the drink could be addictive.

Spain established cacao plantations in its colonies and kept the chocolate-making process that the Maya taught them a secret for almost 100 years. When the Spanish monks who made chocolate revealed the secret, chocolate manufacturing swept through Europe.

> The Aztec called one of their chocolate drinks *xocoatl.* This is where the word *chocolate* comes from.

Today, every day nine out of 10 Americans eat some form of chocolate, according to the Chocolate Manufacturers Association. In addition to chocolate, cacao beans are used in medicine and soft drinks. Cocoa butter pressed from the beans is used in cosmetics.

Chia

Chia is a name for several related plants that are native to the South-west deserts. Their small gray seeds are extremely high in protein. Because they contain all of the essential amino acids, this protein is complete. Chia seeds also contain a substance that helps the body reduce inflammation, boost immunity and lower blood pressure. Indian people raised chia for medicine and food. They made drinks, porridges, and flour from it.

Aztec warriors and hunters lived on chia in the field. American Indian runners also relied on it. When the Spaniards forced Indians to march long distances to the California missions, the Indians survived by eating the seeds and drinking a small amount of water. This was possible because each chia seed absorbs more than 12 times its weight in water. In water a substance inside the seed forms a gel. (Moist seeds are anchored in desert soil because of this.) When Indian people drank chia in water, their bodies conserved water. Today chia is grown as a food crop.

▲▽▲▽▲▽▲▽▲▽▲▽▲▽▲▽▲▽▲▽▲▽▲▽▲▽▲

FLOWERS

Indian people of South America grew flowers for food. Nasturtiums produce flowers that are yellow, orange, or red. Quecha farmers of the Andes grew them as vegetables, which they cooked and ate raw in salads.

Both the Inca and Aztec grew flowers for the beauty their blooms provided. The Inca planted petunias. The Aztec grew zinnias, dahlias, poinsettias, marigolds, and morning glories.

▽▲▽▲▽▲▽▲▽▲▽▲▽▲▽▲▽▲▽▲▽▲▽▲▽▲▽

Jerusalem Artichokes

Jerusalem artichokes are the roots of a type of sunflower. They were planted and harvested by Indians of the Southeast. Their nutritional value compares to that of potatoes. Today they are found in the produce section of many grocery stores.

Jicama

Jicama is a root crop that was first grown by the Indian people of Mesoamerica. It is shaped like a large turnip and has a cool, sweet flavor. Raw jicama is crunchy and is often used in salads today.

Pawpaws

Pawpaws are fruits that grow on trees native to the hardwood forests of the Northeast. American Indians from a number of tribes cultivated pawpaw trees. Today scientists use substances in the tree's twigs to develop anticancer drugs.

Peanuts or Groundnuts

Peanuts are native to South America. American Indians began raising them at least 6,000 years ago in the Andes. Circum-Caribbean Indians also grew them. Peanuts provided them with energy from fat and with protein. (Per ounce, peanuts contain more protein than steak.)

At first Spanish conquistadores did not like peanuts, but they recognized their nutritional value. They took them to West Africa to feed the slaves they had begun to ship throughout the world. Peanuts became an important part of the diet of West African people. The peanuts grown in the United States today were brought from Africa.

Today people in the United States prefer their peanuts roasted. Roasted and ground peanuts are made into peanut butter. Peanut oil is used in salad dressings and for cooking. Peanut shells are used for animal feed, fireplace logs, wallboard, and cat litter. Many products, such as metal polish, bleach, detergent, axle grease, face creams, shaving cream, rubber, cosmetics, paint, shampoo, and medicine, also contain peanuts.

▲▽▲▽▲▽▲▽▲▽▲▽▲▽▲▽▲▽▲▽▲▽▲▽▲▽▲▽▲▽▲

PEANUT LOVERS

Archaeologists have found plazas covered with peanut shells in the middle of ancient Andean cities. Ancient Peruvians decorated their pottery with peanut designs and even made pots that were shaped like peanuts. People who lived on the western coast of Peru buried their mummies with jars of peanuts.

▽▲▽▲▽▲▽▲▽▲▽▲▽▲▽▲▽▲▽▲▽▲▽▲▽▲▽▲▽▲▽

Pecans and Hickory Nuts

Pecans and Hickory nuts grow on trees. Indians of the Southeast planted them to insure a steady harvest. They used pecans, which contain vitamin E and minerals, to flavor corn cakes. They also removed the oil from pecans to add to deer meat stews.

The Creek (Muskogee) of the Southeast cultivated 11 different varieties of hickory trees. They ate the nuts and made a dye from them.

> The word *pecan* comes from the Algonquian word *pakan*, or *pagan*, which translates as "bone shell."

Pineapples

Pineapples are large, sweet fruit, with yellow flesh and tough skin. They are high in vitamin C. American Indians first grew pineapples in the tropical lowlands of Mesoamerica. Later Circum-Caribbean Indians raised them.

In 1493 when Christopher Columbus landed on what is now the island of Guadeloupe, a party of his men returned to the ship

Pineapples were such a curiosity in Europe that the English rented them to use as centerpieces at their dinner parties. *(PhotoDisc)*

▲▽▲▽▲▽▲▽▲▽▲▽▲▽▲▽▲▽▲▽▲▽▲▽▲▽▲▽

PINEAPPLE

The pineapple's botanical name, *Ananas,* comes from the Tupi-Guarani Indian language. It means "fragrant, delicious fruit." Its common name comes from the Spanish explorers who named it *piña* because they thought it looked like a pine cone.

▽▲▽▲▽▲▽▲▽▲▽▲▽▲▽▲▽▲▽▲▽▲▽▲▽▲▽▲▽

with pineapples. Later the Portuguese took the fruits from Brazil to their other colonies. Large pineapple plantations were eventually established in South America, Hawaii, Formosa, the Philippines, and Australia.

Tomatoes

Tomatoes are round fruit with an acidic taste. They are high in vitamin C and A as well as fiber. Indians of Mesoamerica and the Andes grew them. The name *tomato* comes from the Aztec, who called them *tomatl.*

In 1527 Spanish conquistadores returned to southern Europe with tomato seeds that produced yellow fruit. Southern Europeans called tomatoes love apples because they believed that people who ate them attracted love. Other Europeans thought tomatoes were poisonous. Early English colonists to New England brought seeds with them but grew tomatoes only for decoration. Today the United States is

▲▽▲▽▲▽▲▽▲▽▲▽▲▽▲▽▲▽▲▽▲▽▲▽▲▽▲

TROPICAL FRUITS

Tropical fruits filled the orchards planted by Indians of Mesoamerica and South America. Juice from three of these fruits is used in many blended fruit drinks today:

Guava is a sweet fruit that contains large amounts of vitamin C and A as well as an enzyme that helps with digestion. Indians began planting these trees about 2,000 years ago in Mesoamerica, South America, and the Circum-Caribbean.

Papayas are sweet fruits that grow on plants so large that they resemble trees. Indian farmers people in Mesoamerica and the Circum-Caribbean cultivated them. Indian people ate papayas and used them to treat insect bites and for indigestion.

Passion fruit grows on vines in the South American tropics. These fruits contain sweet pulp and thousands of tiny seeds. They are very high in vitamin C. The Inca of South America grew passion fruit.

▽▲▽▲▽▲▽▲▽▲▽▲▽▲▽▲▽▲▽▲▽▲▽▲▽▲▽

the largest tomato grower in the world. Each person in the United States eats about 18 pounds of fresh tomatoes and 70 pounds of processed tomatoes annually.

Vanilla

Vanilla plants are a type of orchid that is native to Mesoamerica. Indian farmers cultivated vanilla and pollinated the flowers by hand. They also invented a way to cure or age the vanilla seeds and turn the essential oil they contain into a flavor.

The Maya and the Aztec developed this process. First they wilted the beans to produce the substances that give vanilla its flavor. Then they heated them to speed flavor production and keep them from spoiling. This also turned them a dark brown color. Next they dried the pods. Finally they conditioned them by putting them in closed boxes and kept them there for about three months.

Mesoamerican cooks used vanilla to flavor chocolate. Vanilla was considered so valuable that the Aztec paid their taxes with it. Today, vanilla is grown in tropical countries throughout the world. The largest crop of vanilla comes from the state of Veracruz in Mexico. There the Totonac Indian people continue to grow the plants as they have for centuries.

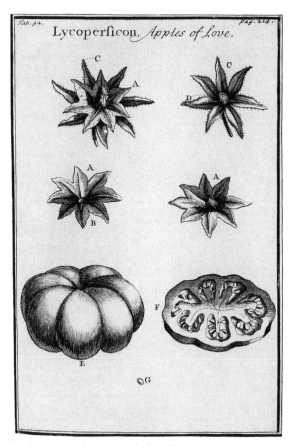

At first many Europeans believed tomatoes were poisonous. Others believed that giving someone a tomato would make that person fall in love with the gift bearer. In this illustration from *The Compleat Herbal* printed in England between 1719 and 1730, tomatoes were called apples of love. *(Library of Congress, Prints and Photographs Division [LC-USZ62-95197])*

A SECRET PROCESS

Spaniards took vanilla pods back to Spain in the 1500s, but the Indian people kept their method for making vanilla flavoring a secret. Europeans could not figure out how to make it into flavoring for more than 200 years.

Yams

Yams are plants with climbing vines with heart-shaped leaves. They produce underground tubers that form buds. These buds grow new plants. Yams, which are a different plant than sweet potatoes, can grow to enormous size—as long as six feet and weighing up to 150 pounds. American Indian farmers of the tropics grew many varieties of yams. Today yams continue to be a source of nutrition in tropical areas throughout the world. They are also used by the pharmaceutical industry to make synthetic steroids.

Yucca

Yucca is a plant that is native to the northern part of what is now Mexico, arid regions of Mesoamerica, and the deserts of North America. The plants grow up to 40 feet tall and consist of a woody stem surrounded by tufts of long, stiff leaves. Indigenous people living in the Southwest, Baja California, and the northern deserts of Mexico used yucca plants they had gathered for food, medicine, and fiber.

Southwest American Indians ate the petals of yucca flowers raw or in salads and boiled as a vegetable. Yucca fruits were also commonly used to make beverages by a number of tribes. They peeled and roasted them and also dried them for winter storage. The Apache mixed piñon nuts with yucca fruit to make a pudding. They also boiled them into a syrup that they brushed on other vegetables they were drying.

While not a popular food item for non-Indians today, the yucca's roots are used in the production of some root beers. Yucca is grown throughout the warm regions of the United States as a decorative ornamental.

▲▼▲▼▲▼▲▼▲▼▲▼▲▼▲▼▲▼▲▼▲▼▲▼▲▼▲▼▲

FRUIT ROLLS

The Navajo (Dineh) and Pueblo peoples removed seeds from ripe yucca fruit. Then they boiled the fruits into thick jam that they shaped into rolls and ate throughout the winter. These were possibly the world's first fruit roll-ups.

▼▲▼▲▼▲▼▲▼▲▼▲▼▲▼▲▼▲▼▲▼▲▼▲▼▲▼▲▼

ANIMALS THAT AMERICAN INDIANS RAISED

Although no large animals native to the Americas were suitable for domestication, American Indians raised smaller animals and birds for the meat that they provided. These included dogs, guinea pigs, Muscovy ducks, llamas, and turkeys. The Maya of Mesoamerica kept bees in hives next to their homes.

Bees

Bees are insects that produce honey and wax. The Maya of Mesoamerica domesticated stingless bees. Indian beekeepers cut tree trunks containing nests of wild bees and put the hives near their houses. They learned what types of plants bees needed to make the best honey. Later they began building shelters that contained from 100 to 200 hives. Maya beekeepers bred many varieties of stingless bees.

The Spaniards were impressed by Maya bee yards that consisted of thousands of hives. Later they tried to stop local honey production because it competed with their own sugarcane plantations. Because the Catholic Church needed more beeswax for candles than Spain could provide, the Spaniards changed their minds and encouraged beekeeping.

Dogs

Dogs were domesticated and were occasionally used for food throughout the Americas. The Aztec bred hairless dogs called *xoloitzcuintlis* for this purpose. They fed them avocados, corn, and meat to fatten them. The Spanish priest Father Bernardo Sahagún wrote that the dogs were good to eat. Other Spaniards, including Hernán Cortés and his crew, butchered so many as food supplies for their ships that the breed nearly became extinct.

Guinea Pigs

Guinea pigs are small, burrowing rodents. Indians of South America domesticated them thousands of years ago as a source of meat. These animals breed rapidly. Ten females and one male could produce about 77 pounds of high-protein, low-fat meat in a year. The Inca, who called them *cuy,* kept guinea pigs in their homes and fed them table scraps. Today cuy continues to be a favorite dish in Peru.

SESTA CALLE
CORO·TASQVE

Indian people living in what is now Peru began domesticating llamas in about 5000 B.C. *(After Felipe Guamán Poma de Ayala.* Nueva corónica y buen gobierno)

Llamas

Llamas are fur-bearing animals of the camel family. Indian people of the Andes raised them for food and fiber as well as to carry burdens. The Inca ate fresh and dried llama meat. Early Spanish explorers wrote of seeing storehouses full of *charqui,* or dried llama meat. *Charqui* is the native word from which the modern word *jerky* is derived.

At first Spanish conquistadores ate llama meat. Later they encouraged Indian herders to raise cattle and sheep instead. Indian people continued to raise llamas, although not in the number they had before conquest.

Muscovy Ducks

Muscovy ducks are the largest breed of ducks in the world. Mesoamerican farmers raised them for food. Spaniards wrote little about the domestication of ducks by Indian farmers, but they took the ducks to Europe. There they became the most popular duck raised. More than 70 percent of ducks eaten in Europe today are Muscovy ducks. They are prized for their unique flavor and because they are relatively low in fat.

Turkeys

Turkeys are large birds whose flesh is low in fat and high in protein. Ancient people of Mesoamerica domesticated them and valued them so much that they paid taxes with turkeys. Later the Anasazi of the Southwest raised them too. The Anasazi bred turkeys to control feather color. They kept different types of turkeys in separate areas so that they would not crossbreed. Although they ate turkey, the Anasazi valued the birds more for their feathers, which they wove into robes. They also used the tame birds to eat insect pests.

Father Bernardo de Sahagún, a Spanish priest, who tasted turkey wings prepared by Aztec cooks, wrote that turkeys were the "master of meat." "It is tasty, fat and savory," he said of the bird. Between 1498 and 1511, Spanish explorers took turkeys to Europe, where they became popular.

This wild turkey from Arizona could very well be one of the descendants of turkeys the ancient Anasazi bred and raised hundreds of years ago. *(Gary M. Stolz/U.S. Fish and Wildlife Service)*

TIME LINE	
3500 B.C.	Indians of the Andes begin domesticating the llama.
3400 to 2300 B.C.	Indian farmers of Mesoamerica domesticate the avocado.
3000 B.C.	Circum-Caribbean Indians cultivate peanuts.
750 B.C.	South American farmers begin growing avocados.
200 B.C.	Mesoamerican farmers domesticate turkeys.
100 B.C. to A.D. 800	Maya farmers of Mesoamerica domesticate Muscovy ducks.
A.D. 1	The Maya of Mesoamerica invent chocolate.
A.D. 700	Farmers of Mesoamerica and South America grow tomatoes.

Food Preservation and Storage

American Indian hunters, gatherers, or farmers needed to preserve their food. Preservation techniques that kept food edible for months allowed them to eat when game was scarce and to obtain nutrition from plants throughout the winter.

Once they had preserved food, they needed to store it in a way that would keep it safe from hungry animals and insects. Indians throughout the Americas came up with a number of effective ways to do this. Early European colonists copied many of these techniques from the Indian people they encountered.

FOOD PRESERVATION

Indians of North America, Mesoamerica, and South America relied on several methods to preserve food. Drying food was the most frequently used method. Drying food helps to keep it edible for a long time. When moisture is removed from food, microorganisms that cause it to spoil dry right along with the food. These food-spoiling agents have a difficult time living and reproducing. In many cases the microorganisms in food die as a result of drying.

Sun Drying

Indians preserved meat that they obtained from hunting by cutting it into very thin slices and then drying it on frames or racks. Today, meat that has been dried in this manner is called jerky. Jerky, a high-energy snack food, is sold in many stores today.

Drying meat kept it good to eat for a long time. It also made it easier to carry. This was very important for tribes that relied on hunting and gathering, such as those of the Great Plains. Because these people traveled long distances in order to follow game, their food needed to be both compact and lightweight. Strips of meat that had been dried would last up to three years and weighed only about a sixth as much as fresh meat did.

Indian people of North America often pounded the jerky that they had made into powder. Then they mixed it with dried berries and animal fat. Occasionally they added nuts to this mixture. This served as a high-energy trail food for American Indian travelers and was an important source of calories, iron, and vitamin C during the winter-

Dried meat, or jerky, hangs on a drying rack in the camp of Plains buffalo hunters photographed in 1871. *(Photograph No. NWDNS-165-A1-15/National Archives and Records Administration–College Park)*

time. Each tribe had a slightly different recipe and called the food by a different name. Most people today call it pemmican.

Indians made and stored pemmican in rawhide containers called parfleches. When they had filled the containers with powdered meat and dry berries, they poured enough melted animal fat over the mixture to coat each fiber of the meat. Then they sewed the bags shut with sinew. Before the fat cooled and became solid, they walked on the bags to compress the pemmican. This last step squeezed out the air along with airborne microorganisms that could cause spoilage. It also made the bundles smaller so that they were more convenient to

▲▽▲▽▲▽▲▽▲▽▲▽▲▽▲▽▲▽▲▽▲▽▲▽▲▽▲

TRAIL FOOD

The word *pemmican* comes from the Cree *pimikkan* from *pimmi*, which means fat or grease. It was made part of the English language in the late 1700s by colonists who learned to make this trail food from the Indians and carried it with them as they explored North America.

▼▲▼▲▼▲▼▲▼▲▼▲▼▲▼▲▼▲▼▲▼▲▼▲▼▲▼

store. Prepared and packaged in this way pemmican could last for years. According to some reports, it could still be eaten up to 30 years later.

European trappers, traders, and soldiers ate this Indian food on the frontier. In most cases they did not make their own pemmican. Instead they traded with the Indians for it at forts and posts. They called pemmican bags "pieces." In time, making pemmican became a booming business for American Indians and a few non-Indian entrepreneurs.

In addition to drying berries for pemmican, American Indians dried a number of other fruits. They also dried such vegetables as green corn and squash. The Hidatsa, who farmed along what is now the Missouri River in North Dakota, dried vegetables in the fields where they grew them. They built outdoor drying stages, or platforms, of wood to keep corn and squash well above the reach of animals. These platforms allowed air to circulate so that the food could dry. During rains, they placed hides over the top of the stages to protect the food.

Fire Drying

In climates where rain was common, American Indians built fires beneath the platforms to hurry the vegetable drying process. They also dried meat in this way. American Indian tribes of the Northwest Pacific Coast dried salmon with fires. They hung the fish on racks made from a number of poles tied together. Sometimes when they were finished, they pounded the dried fish into powder in order to make it easier to store.

Indians living in the Plateau region of North America dug roots from many varieties of plants, including biscuit root, bitter root, and a type of camas. Flathead (Salish), Kalispell, Spokan, and Nez Perce Indians washed and peeled the roots before they dried them. Sometimes they roasted the roots in a large pit that was lined with rocks. First they built a fire and let it burn until the rocks were extremely hot. When the fire died down, the Indians placed leaves and grass on top of the rocks. After this they put the roots they wanted to dry on top of the leaves. Then they covered them with mats woven from fiber and finally with earth.

Once the roots had been roasted, women pounded them into flour. Often they mixed this flour with dried elk or deer meat, berries, and animal fat or fish oil to make pemmican. Until they were ready to use the roots they had preserved, they put them in parfleches. They stored these on platforms in trees where they would be safe from hungry animals.

American Indians of farming tribes of the Northeast, Great Plains, and Mesoamerica preserved green, or fresh, corn by parching it. They cut the soft kernels from the cob and placed them into clay bowls that they then set on a fire. Because the kernels had been cut, they were open at the bottom and swelled up without popping. This parched corn resembled the food popularly called corn nuts today. Indians often carried parched corn with them when they traveled.

American Indians of the Northeast mixed parched corn with maple syrup to sweeten it. This provided them with quick food energy when they traveled. The Aztec of Mesoamerica called their parched corn *pinolli*. Pinolli is sold in the Mexican food sections of some grocery stores.

> The Hidatsa of the Great Plains parched green corn by spearing an ear on a stick and holding it over a fire.

Smoking

The smoke from the fires that American Indian people built beneath drying racks kept insects away when the racks were covered with meat, vegetables, or fruit. American Indians learned that wet wood produced a great deal of smoke and that certain kinds of wood gave meat and fish a distinctive flavor. Plains Indians sometimes smoked meat over a fire and afterward let it air-dry for several days. American Indians of the Northwest and Plateau regions smoked salmon. In addition to flavoring meats and fish, the smoke also helped to preserve them. Smoke contains substances called phenols that slow the growth of microorganisms, which cause food to spoil.

Freeze-drying

More than a thousand years ago the Inca, who lived in what is now Peru, discovered how to freeze-dry food. They invented the same basic process that is used today to freeze-dry instant potatoes and coffee. Freeze-drying gives food a shelf life of several years.

Although the Inca freeze-dried llama meat and a number of vegetables, their main use of freeze-drying was to preserve sweet and white potatoes. Freeze-drying also made potatoes easier to transport and store. When they had harvested the potatoes, the Inca arranged them on the ground and left them overnight to freeze. After cold

▲▼▲▼▲▼▲▼▲▼▲▼▲▼▲▼▲▼▲▼▲▼▲▼▲▼▲▼▲▼▲

FREEZE-DRYING FACTS

When ice changes directly into a gas without first melting to become water, moisture is quickly and effectively removed from food. Freeze-drying helps food keep much of its flavor that would be lost if the food were air-dried.

Today freeze-drying is used on about 400 foods, including vegetables, meat, and dairy products, such as cheese for boxed macaroni-and-cheese dinners. It is also used to preserve flowers.

▼▲▼▲▼▲▼▲▼▲▼▲▼▲▼▲▼▲▼▲▼▲▼▲▼▲▼▲▼▲▼

mountain temperatures froze the potatoes, the water inside slowly vaporized under the low air pressure. Each night the potatoes froze again, losing more and more moisture. The Inca speeded this process by repeatedly walking over the potatoes to squeeze out even more moisture.

They left some of the freeze-dried potatoes whole and ground others into potato flour that was used as the basis of a kind of bread. This flour could be stored for a very long time. When the Inca reconstituted potatoes in water, they used them in soups and stews as well as in bread. Freeze-dried potatoes are an important part of the diet of Indians of the Andes today.

In addition to potatoes, the Inca freeze-dried meat and other vegetables, including nasturtiums, a type of flower. Most non-Indians ignored freeze-drying for hundreds of years. It finally gained acceptance outside the Andes when scientists used it to preserve blood plasma during World War II. In the 1960s food companies began making freeze-dried meals for campers. Instant potato flakes and freeze-dried coffee were the first products to be marketed in grocery stores.

Preserving in Oil

Indians who lived along the northern and central Pacific coast preserved food by covering it with oil. Because the Northwest has a rainy climate, air-drying food was not practical for them. The oil kept food good to eat by serving as a barrier against microorganisms

> Another name for eulachon is candlefish. They were called this because they contained so much oil that Indians of the Northwest put wicks in dried eulachon and burned them to provide light.

that cause mold. These tiny organisms need oxygen in order to grow. Indians of the Northwest obtained the oil from eulachon, a fish that contains about 20 percent oil.

After catching the fish in nets, the Indians stored them in pits until they began to decompose. This ripening stage helped to release the oil that the fish contained. Next the Indians placed the fish in large wooden boxes filled with water. Then they dropped red-hot stones into the water to make it boil. When the fish oil rose to the surface of the water, they skimmed it off and used it to cover berries stored in smaller wooden boxes that they had made especially for this purpose.

In the Northeast the Beothuk, who lived in what is now New-foundland, heated caribou fat, skimmed off the impurities, and stored it in birch-bark boxes. They also heated seal blubber to turn it into oil. They stored this in animal bladders.

CROP STORAGE

Once they had preserved the food that they grew, hunted, or gathered American Indians needed to find safe places to store it. Tribes in Mesoamerica, South, and North America devised ingenious ways to store food. Inside their homes American Indians temporarily stored small amounts of food in pottery bowls and jars, baskets, and boxes made from rawhide or bark. They stored food that needed to be kept cool in streams and caves. They cached larger amounts of food on platforms and in storage bins and granaries.

Cold Storage

One of the earliest methods that American Indians used for storing meat was to keep it in a stream. Archaeologists have found evidence that Ice Age hunters cached mastodon meat underwater in what are now Michigan, Ohio, Indiana, and New York. To learn how long this storage method would keep meat fresh, archaeologists put large pieces of meat in a shallow pond and in peat bogs. (Peat is a deposit of partly decomposed plants and is high in acid content.) The meat remained fresh through the winter. In the spring, although the meat was discolored on the outside, the inside was edible. The amount of bacteria in the meat that was stored in the water was about the same as that in meat that was stored in a freezer.

The Inuit of the Arctic built small food storage additions to their igloos. These "refrigerators" made from snow and ice kept meat frozen throughout the long winter. The Inuit also dug storage compartments in the permafrost (soil that is always frozen) and used them to store food throughout the year. The Beothuk of Newfoundland removed the bones from the caribou meat that they had hunted and packed the meat into birch-bark boxes. They stacked them in special storage huts throughout the winter.

Early farmers of the Northeast and Southeast kept grain in caves where it would remain cool. They also used cool, dry caves to store seeds that they had saved. When these natural storage lockers were not readily available, they devised other ways to keep both seeds and future food dry and safe.

Inuit fish caches that were built on stilts kept dried food out of the reach of hungry animals. *(Frank and Frances Carpenter Collection/Library of Congress)*

Storage Caches

Sometimes American Indians built food storage caches on stilts in order to keep their food out of the reach of hungry animals and insects. In many instances these storage caches were very simple, but sometimes they were more sophisticated. Early European colonists learned from the Indians how to store corn off the ground. They even copied the way Indians of the Southeast built flared-sided corncribs.

American Indian farmers in the Ohio valley built underground silos that could hold 30 to 40 bushels of shelled corn. They lined these cylindrical storage pits with grass and rawhide and covered them with caps made of grass. Indians of the Northeast dug storage pits about two to three feet in diameter and lined them with bark to keep corn dry and safe from rodents. The Hidatsa of the Great Plains also dug pits and lined them with grass and hides for their corn and dried squash.

Indians sometimes mixed herbs with food when they stored it in order to keep it edible for longer periods of time. Klamath Indians of the Plateau placed yarrow stems, leaves, and flowers inside the cavities of fish that they had cleaned in order to keep them tasting fresh longer than they would without it. (Yarrow contains chemicals that are mildly disinfectant.) Some North American Indians stored mint with dried meat in order to flavor it and to keep it tasting fresh longer as well. The Kootenai of the Northwest packed dried meat and berries with mint to flavor it and to repel insects. The Maya, Aztec, and Inca also stored dried herbs with the food to keep insects away.

▲▽▲▽▲▽▲▽▲▽▲▽▲▽▲▽▲▽▲▽▲▽▲▽▲▽▲▽▲

FOOD THIEVES

American Indian food caches were not safe from Europeans. A few days after the *Mayflower* landed, a party of Pilgrims discovered food that the Indians had stored. "We marched to the place we called Cornhill, where we had found the corn before," one of them wrote in a journal. " At another place we had seen before, we dug and found some more corn, two or three baskets full, and a bag of beans. . . . In all we had about ten bushels, which will be enough for seed. It was with God's help that we found this corn, for how else could we have done it, without meeting some Indians who might trouble us." Far from troubling the English, the Indians provided them with food and taught them, not only how to plant corn, but also how to fertilize it and store it.

▼▲▼▲▼▲▼▲▼▲▼▲▼▲▼▲▼▲▼▲▼▲▼▲▼▲▼▲▼

DEPOCITODELINGA COLLCA

topa ynga yupamqui.

The Inca stored their crops in large stone granaries. From there they were distributed to soldiers and to people in need. (After Felipe Guamán Poma de Ayala. Nueva corónica y buen gobierno)

The Inca made certain that no one in the empire went hungry. In this way they ensured the loyalty of their people. In return, everyone who could work did so, serving in the military or working for the government. Even the blind were given the job of shelling corn before it was stored.

Granaries

American Indians of the Southwest, Mesoamerica, and South America used buildings to store their grain. The Anasazi of the Southwest made adobe-lined storage pits and also built aboveground storerooms along overhangs in canyons. Some archaeologists believe that food storage inspired the Anasazi to build the pueblos where they eventually lived. Anasazi pueblos, such as Mesa Verde in what is now

Colorado and Pueblo Bonito in what is now New Mexico, served as regional food distribution centers. The Anasazi stored thousands of bushels of grain at these pueblos.

In addition to storing corn in aboveground cribs, the Maya of Mesoamerica built large underground bins called *chultunes* for long-term storage. These were bell-shaped and lined with stones. The Aztec of Mesoamerica built aboveground stone granaries too. Rulers stored tributes they collected from farmers in both of these types of warehouses.

The Inca of South America were able to build their empire, the largest one in the pre-Columbian Americas, because of their ability to grow and control food. They carved big warehouses into the sides of mountains. There mountain breezes could cool food. They also built stone granaries in cities. Their storage facilities, called *colca*, were spaced about every 100 miles along the roads the Inca built. The warehouses were filled by farmers who were required to work for a certain period of time growing crops on state-owned lands. This work tax was called *mita*.

Spanish conquistadores under the command of Francisco Pizarro reported that potato flour, quinoa, corn, and dried fish and llama meat filled these storehouses to their ceilings. Some of the harvest fed Inca royalty and government workers. Much of the food was saved in case of crop failure. It was also distributed to the elderly and the disabled who could not work to feed themselves.

The food storage system of the Inca was so effective that when Pizarro and his men landed in what is now Peru, they were able to raid the storehouses for food. They also found cloth, sandals, tools, and military weapons there. Well fed and well supplied, they were able to overthrow the Inca and rule the land and the Indian people who had worked so hard to farm it.

How American Indians Cooked and What They Ate

American Indians cooked much of the food they hunted, gathered, and grew. In fact, the people of the Arctic were the only people of the Americas who did not do much cooking. Wood for fueling fires was scarce in the North. Often the only fuel the Inuit people had was seal or whale oil to use in their lamps that provided light and heat through the long winters. Cooking would have wasted precious fuel. They ate about half of their fish and meat raw.

COOKING METHODS

Indians of the Americas did not use metal cooking pots or frying pans, because iron deposits did not lie close to the surface of the Earth in the Americas. Instead, Indian cooks invented many ways to prepare meals without them.

Roasting and Barbecuing

The earliest and most basic American Indian cooking method was to spear meat or vegetables on green sticks and hold them over an open fire. This required a great deal of time standing by the fire, so cooks built grilling racks. They made them out of green wood that did not easily burn when it was set over the fire.

The Taino people of the Caribbean introduced grilling racks to Europeans. The Spanish called the cooking method *barbacoa*. Today barbecues are an important part of southern cooking and a popular warm-weather cooking method throughout the United States.

When foods took a long time to cook, even green wood caught fire. Indian cooks met this challenge by heating rocks until they glowed. They grilled their food over these rocks rather than a fire. American Indians of what is now Louisiana and Florida used dried clay cooking balls that were about the size of tennis balls. They heated them and placed up to 200 in a roasting pit.

Boiling

Some American Indians boiled food in a hole that they dug in the earth. They lined it with an animal hide from which they had removed the fur. Then they filled the skin with water and dropped heated cooking stones into it. When the water began to cool, they added more hot stones. Tribes of the Great Plains and Great Basin region used this method to boil meat and make soups and stews.

Indians in many parts of the Americas grilled fish and meat on racks set over fires. This picture was made by John White sometime between 1562 and 1565 in what is now Florida. *(Library of Congress, Prints and Photographs Division [LC-USZ62-581])*

Hunting and gathering people, who traveled a great deal, also boiled food in portable containers that they sewed from hide. Indian cooks fastened these hide bags to wooden tripods and filled them with meat, vegetables, and water. Then they added heated stones to cook the food.

American Indians who settled in one place invented other kinds of cooking equipment. Some made large, sturdy jars in which they could stone-boil food. Northeast and Southeast American Indians carved cooking vessels from soapstone (steatite). Sometimes they stone-boiled food in boxes made of birch bark. Indian people of the Northwest constructed large wooden boxes for the same purpose. California Indians, including the Yurok and Pomo peoples, were skilled basket makers. They made cooking baskets that were water-tight and had flared sides so that they could easily remove the rocks when the meal had finished cooking.

Steaming and Slow Cooking

Indians throughout the Americas sometimes dug a pit and lined it with stones. Then they built a fire inside of this depression. When

▲▼▲▼▲▼▲▼▲▼▲▼▲▼▲▼▲▼▲▼▲▼▲▼▲▼

CLAMBAKES

Indians of the Northeast invented the clambake. They taught colonists to put seaweed on hot rocks in a pit and cover it with clams and corn. The settlers adopted the clambake. Today it is a New England tradition.

▼▲▼▲▼▲▼▲▼▲▼▲▼▲▼▲▼▲▼▲▼▲▼▲▼

the rocks were hot, they scooped out the coals and put wet grass or leaves on the rocks. They covered this layer with food and then covered the food with another layer of grass or leaves. After this they poured water into the pit to make steam. Then they quickly covered the opening with hide and heaped earth on it to weigh it down. Several hours later the food inside the pit was completely cooked.

Griddle Cooking

Indians in many parts of the Americas made flat cakes and bread from ground corn, nuts, or seeds that they mixed with water. They poured this batter onto a heated griddle stone. When one side of the bread was done cooking, they turned it over, much as pancakes are made today.

At first Indian cooks used flat stones found in nature as griddles. Later they improved on them. Indians of the Northeast carved baking stones from soapstone. Indians of the Southwest used basalt, a type of volcanic rock, on which they made a thin corn bread called piki bread. They ground and polished the cooking surface and coated it with oil so that the bread would not stick. In the Amazon Basin and the Circum-Caribbean, cooks made unleavened manioc bread on flat stones. Aztec cooks used stone griddles that they called *comalli* to cook tortillas.

COOKING EQUIPMENT
Grinders

Before Indians could cook seeds, nuts, or grains, they had to grind them. Hunters and gatherers pounded seeds between rocks. Mesoamerican and southwestern cooks used a mano and metate to grind corn into meal. They rubbed the mano, or grinding stone, over corn heaped on a flat stone called a metate. (Mesoamerican cooks also used a rough-surfaced mortar made of volcanic rock to grind tomatoes and chilies.) American Indians of the Northeast and Southeast pounded corn into meal by placing it in a wooden bucket and

▲▼▲▼▲▼▲▼▲▼▲▼▲▼▲▼▲▼▲▼▲▼▲▼▲▼▲▼▲

PELLAGRA

Europeans did not know that they needed to process corn in order to release the niacin, as American Indians did. Non-Indians who relied on corn as a major part of their diets began to get sick. They had dry and scaly skin, diarrhea, vomiting, and saw and heard things that were not there. In Italy, this disease was called *pellagra,* and in Africa it was called *mealies*. Not until 1914 did modern medicine discover that pellagra is caused by not getting enough niacin.

▼▲▼▲▼▲▼▲▼▲▼▲▼▲▼▲▼▲▼▲▼▲▼▲▼▲▼▲▼

pounding it with the end of a log. Often they used a sapling, or young, small tree, as a spring to help lift the log. This made their work easier. New England colonists borrowed this idea and placed a communal corn pounder like those used by the Indians in the central squares of their villages.

Before they ground corn, American Indians of the Northeast and Southeast soaked it in a mixture of water and ashes. Indians of Mesoamerica and the Southwest soaked corn in a mixture of water and ground limestone to make hominy. This soaking separated the bond between vitamin B₃, or niacin, and starch in the corn so that the body could use it. Indian meal was more like hominy grits than cornmeal that is sold in grocery stores today.

Popcorn Poppers

Indians throughout the Americas ate popcorn for thousands of years before Europeans arrived. (Corn contains some moisture in the starchy interior of the kernel. When heated, this moisture expands, creating enough pressure to cause the starch to explode, causing the corn to pop.) At first the Indians popped corn by throwing

American Indians of the Northeast used log mortars to pound corn that had been soaked in water and wood ashes. This picture of an Iroquois man making corn meal was taken in 1912. *(National Archives of Canada/PA181637/R. F. Waugh Collection)*

Although American Indians sometimes popped corn by placing ears into a fire, a more convenient way was to fill a popper with hot sand and corn kernels. *(A96664/Field Museum)*

kernels onto hot coals or pushing a stick through the cob and toasting a whole ear over a fire. Later they invented clay pots to hold hot sand that they scooped from beneath a fire. They added popcorn kernels and stirred them until they popped.

The Arawak people traded popcorn with the crew of Christopher Columbus's ships. Indians of the Northeast brought popcorn for British colonists during peace negotiations as a goodwill offering. Sometimes Northeast Indians stirred maple syrup into popcorn to make a kind of caramel corn.

Cooking and Eating Utensils

Indians of the Americas served food in pottery bowls or tightly woven baskets. They stored small amounts of food in pottery jars, baskets, animal bladders, and in wooden, bark, or hide boxes. The containers that they used depended on the materials they had and the food they were storing.

Indian cooks carved cooking spoons, paddles, and ladles from bone, horn, or wood. Sometimes they used gourds for utensils. The Maya made colanders by drilling holes in large gourds called calabashes. Indians throughout the Americas made bowls and cups from dried gourds.

AMERICAN INDIAN CUISINE

Indians of the Americas combined the foods that they prepared in a number of creative ways. The distinctive regional dishes that they invented influenced cooking throughout the world. In the Americas European colonists adopted American Indian cuisines, or cooking styles, into their diets.

North American Cuisine

Indians of North Americas prepared a wide variety of foods. Many dishes eaten throughout the United States today were first created by

Northeast and Southeast American Indian cooks. For example, Indians taught colonists to make thick corn flatbread. Northeastern and southeastern colonists sometimes called it corn pone, johnny-cake, or journey cakes.

The Iroquois of the Northeast also made a boiled corn bread and a cornmeal mush, often sweetened with maple syrup. When the colonists adopted this mush, they called it Indian pudding. Sometimes Iroquois cooks added berries to cornmeal dumplings or ate them with corn syrup. Colonists reported they used clear, sweet syrup from corn stalks to sweeten their food. They increased the sugar content of the stalks by removing the newly developed ears from the corn they had planted. Indian cooks also used cornmeal to make samp, a porridge that contained beans and dried meat as well as corn. European colonists learned to make samp with beef instead of game.

Northeast Indians taught European colonists to bake beans and sweeten them with maple syrup. They also prepared succotash, a mixture of corn and beans. Often they added game meats or fish to

The people who lived in what is now Peru were expert farmers who grew a number of crops. This drawing, after one by Felipe Guamán Poma de Ayala, depicts Inca corn harvesters in the early 1600s. (Nueva corónica y buen gobierno)

SNACK FOODS

In addition to jerky, popcorn, and caramel corn, American Indians invented other snack foods that are popular today. They ate roasted sunflower seeds by the handful. Indians of Mesoamerica ate parched squash and pumpkin seeds. Throughout the Americas, Indians parched corn. This snack resembled today's corn nuts. Indians of the Northeast mixed ground parched corn with maple sugar to carry as trail food on journeys. New England colonists, who learned how to parch and grind corn from the Iroquois, ate this trail food with milk as a breakfast cereal.

▲▽▲▽▲▽▲▽▲▽▲▽▲▽▲▽▲▽▲▽▲▽▲▽▲▽▲▽▲

THANKSGIVING

Chief Massasoit and the 90 Wampanoag men with him brought five deer to the Thanksgiving feast eaten with the Pilgrims of Plymouth Colony in 1621. In addition to roasted venison, Thanksgiving dinner probably included corn and ducks, geese, or turkey. Beyond that, dried raspberries, strawberries, grapes, plums, cherries, blueberries, or gooseberries could have been on the menu as well. Fish, clams, lobsters, honey, maple syrup, beans, and nuts are other possible foods the Indians and Puritans may have eaten. Cranberries probably were not, because colonists did not learn to boil them with sugar until the 1670s. Although they may have eaten squash or a pumpkin pudding, they did not eat pie.

▽▲▽▲▽▲▽▲▽▲▽▲▽▲▽▲▽▲▽▲▽▲▽▲▽▲▽▲▽

this thick boiled soup. The Narragansett, who showed colonists how to make the dish, called it *msickquatash.*

American Indians had a major influence on southern cooking. They taught colonists to fry corn bread by dropping spoonfuls of cornmeal dough into hot bear fat. These later became known as hush puppies. Indian porridge made from hominy grits became a favorite breakfast food in the South and is still served today. American Indians also introduced southern colonists to pecans, the essential ingredient in pecan pie.

The Choctaw, who lived in what are now Mississippi and Alabama, used dried, ground sassafras leaves to thicken soups and stews. They taught southern settlers to make a sassafras-thickened dish called filé gumbo. It is often made from vegetables, shrimp, and crabs. Filé gumbo has become a famous part of Cajun cuisine.

Mesoamerican Cuisine

Maya and Aztec cooks used cornmeal to make tortillas. Tortillas, thin unleavened bread, are eaten in Mexico today and are part of southwest-

This drawing of Mesoamerican women grinding corn with a mano and metate was made in about 1575.
(Library of Congress, Prints and Photographs Collection [LC-USZ62-113049])

ern regional cooking. Aztec cooks added turkey eggs or honey to the batter sometimes, and they made tortillas from amaranth as well as corn. They wrapped tortillas around a variety of foods. These included chili sauce, tomatoes, mushrooms, squash, and avocados. These were the ancestors of tacos, burritos, enchiladas, and tortilla wraps.

The Aztec also dipped tortillas into a mixture of chilies, tomatoes, and ground pumpkin seeds. Sometimes they heated this mixture, but often they served it cold. The Spanish called it *salsa,* their word for sauce. Indian cooks began using onions and garlic in salsa after Spaniards introduced them to these foods.

Maya cooks made tamales, cornmeal dough wrapped around a filling and steamed in leaves or cornhusks. They filled tamales with meat, fish, ground and toasted squash seeds, greens, black beans, or turkey eggs. The Aztec, who used amaranth as well as corn for tamale dough, used these fillings too. They also filled tamales with mushrooms, prickly pear tunas, rabbit, tomatoes, corn, fish, or chilies. They made fruit tamales and honey tamales as a dessert. Tamales remain a Mexican dish today.

Mesoamerican cooks combined cornmeal and water to make porridge. They spiced it with chili peppers or sweetened it with honey and ate it for breakfast. They made a similar dish with more water and used it as a drink, which they flavored with chocolate and chilies.

> The Aztec invented the mixture of mashed avocados and tomatoes that is known as guacamole. They called it *huaca-mulli.*

▲▼▲▼▲▼▲▼▲▼▲▼▲▼▲▼▲▼▲▼▲▼▲▼▲▼▲▼▲

FLAVORINGS

Mesoamerican, South American, and Circum-Caribbean cooks flavored their food with allspice. They made it by drying and grinding seeds that they gathered from a kind of evergreen tree. Today allspice is used in pies and other baked goods. They also used achiote, which is used today as a food coloring and to flavor Mexican dishes. Mesoamerican cooks sweetened their food with honey and with syrup made from corn stalks or agave plants. Throughout the Americas, Indian people gathered salt from deposits on the ground or evaporated seawater to obtain it.

▼▲▼▲▼▲▼▲▼▲▼▲▼▲▼▲▼▲▼▲▼▲▼▲▼▲▼▲▼

American Indians of Mesoamerica roasted yams with honey to make a similar dish to candied yams eaten today.

In addition to corn, beans played an important role in Mesoamerican cuisine. Cooks soaked and then boiled or baked them. The Maya ate beans cooked with chili peppers. Sometimes Mesoamerican cooks added greens to the beans they boiled. They also parched beans and ground them into flour. Then they added water before they cooked them.

The Maya and Aztec boiled squash or baked it with honey. Sometimes they used squash as an ingredient in stews. They ate squash flowers, shoots, and leaves as vegetables. Raw and toasted squash seeds served as ingredients in many of the dishes they ate.

South American Cuisine

Indian cooks of the Andes made a number of dishes from potatoes. They used flour that they ground from freeze-dried potatoes to make flat bread. Another way that they cooked potatoes was to boil and mash them, adding spices and a bit of fat. Today mashed is one of the most popular ways to prepare this vegetable throughout the world.

Cooks who lived in what is now Peru slow-cooked a dish called *pachamanca* in a pit heated by rocks. This consisted of corn, potatoes, and meat—usually llama or guinea pig. Like cooks in other parts of the Americas, Andean cooks grilled their food on racks over fires. A favorite combination was guinea pig and potatoes.

The Inca made many dishes from the ground quinoa seeds. They combined quinoa meal and water to make a baked flat bread and for tamales. Inca cooks steamed balls of quinoa flour that had been mixed with fat, salt, and seasonings to make a type of dumpling. They cooked quinoa flour, water, and honey into a sweet gruel or porridge. Combined with water, ground quinoa also was used for a high-energy drink. The Inca cooked whole quinoa seeds in soups and stews in combination with potatoes and chili peppers. They used quinoa leaves in stews or alone as a salad or vegetable.

Cooks of the Amazon Basin made ground manioc meal into flat bread. They made this bread fresh each day to eat alone or to dip into soups and stews. After the bread had dried for several days in the sun it could be stored for several months. Although manioc roots are high in starch and contain little protein, the leaves do contain protein. People of the Amazon boiled them and ate them as a vegetable.

Indian cooks toasted processed manioc roots to make a crunchy food that is now called *farofa* in Brazil. Farofa was eaten plain, mixed with vegetables or cashews, and also used to stuff game. Cooks of the Amazon mixed manioc flour with water to make a cereal that is called farina today. They heated the starch that settled to the bottom of manioc juice and boiled it to make tapioca. Both farina and tapioca are sold in grocery stores throughout the world today.

Amazon Indians heated manioc juice so that it was no longer toxic and cooked wild game in it. The manioc juice tenderized the meat. Other foods prepared by people of the South American tropics included roasted yams and fresh and dried fish.

NEW TRADITIONS

As they became familiar with European foods, Indian cooks found creative ways to include them in their own dishes. Aztec cooks added cheese to their tortilla dishes and casseroles. They mixed onions and cilantro into their salsa. They flavored their guacamole with lemon or lime juice. American Indian cooks in South America began cooking citrus fruits with green vegetables and adding them to seafood dishes.

Throughout the Americas, Indian cooks added carrots and onions to the soups and stews that they had been making for centuries. In addition to cornmeal, they began using wheat flour for breads. North American Indian cooks created fry bread, wheat-flour bread dough that is fried rather than baked.

In the Southwest, Indian cooks began using mutton from sheep introduced by the Spaniards in their stews. Pueblo people baked raised wheat-flour bread in outdoor adobe ovens that they adopted from the Spaniards. Pueblo bread has become a traditional food.

At the same time, American Indian foods changed cooking throughout the world. From Europe and Asia to Africa, cooks began adding American Indian foods such as potatoes, tomatoes, and peppers to their traditional recipes.

Although most northern Europeans did not eat potatoes when they were first introduced, by the 1800s potatoes had become the most important part of the diet of Irish peasants. Now potatoes, an American Indian crop, are considered a traditional food of the Irish. Spaniards took potatoes to their colonies in India and the Philippines.

Tomatoes made their way into Italian cooking to become an essential ingredient in sauces. Italians also added cornmeal to their cuisine, making it into polenta, a side dish sometimes prepared with tomatoes and cheese.

Early European slave traders introduced peanuts and manioc to Africa. Both of these foods became an important part of the West African diet. Cooks there use peanut sauces on meat and in stews. Manioc is the main food eaten by many African people, as well as millions of others who live in tropical regions of the world.

Chinese cooks use chili peppers to add a spicy taste to Szechuan and Mongolian cooking. In India, cooks ground chili peppers and

This 1916 photo shows two Taos Pueblo women baking bread in outdoor ovens called *hornos,* a Spanish word. Pueblo cooks adopted raised wheat bread from the Spaniards. It is now considered a traditional Indian food. *(Photograph No. NWDNS-75-N-PU-106/Records of the Bureau of Indian Affairs/National Archives and Records Administration—College Park)*

Tomatoes have been adopted by cooks throughout the world. From Italian spaghetti sauce to Thai dishes, tomatoes are a popular ingredient in many world cuisines. *(PhotoDisc)*

mixed them with other spices that formed curry powder. Fiery hot curries are now considered traditional Indian cuisine.

European cooks in Hungary and Yugoslavia used dried red sweet peppers to make paprika. This spice is used in goulash and many other traditional eastern European dishes. Sweet peppers are also used by Asian-American cooks, who often use them with pineapple to make sweet-and-sour dishes.

When Americans talk of world cuisines, images of exotic foods and ingredients come to mind, not images of Native American hunters, fishers, farmers, and cooks of the past. Without the anonymous contributions of indigenous Americans, world cuisine would not be as rich and diverse as it is today.

GLOSSARY OF
ANCIENT CULTURES
OF THE AMERICAS

This glossary lists some of the important cultures, empires, and city-states in the Americas before 1492. Many of them existed hundreds or thousands of years before Europeans arrived in the Americas. Archaeologists try to piece together the history of America's ancient people from their buildings and the smaller objects they left behind. They can only make educated guesses based on the artifacts that they find.

The history of ancient America is one of changes. Because of this, modern people often mistakenly think that entire groups of ancient Indian people disappeared. Indian people and their civilizations did not vanish. Governments rose to power, fell, and were replaced by other governments. Sometimes large groups of people moved. They shared ideas with their neighbors and borrowed ideas from them. The Indians who made up civilizations of the past are the ancestors of the Indians of the Americas who are alive today.

Adena   The Adena culture arose along the valleys of the Mississippi and Ohio Rivers and lasted from about 1500 B.C. to A.D. 200. Adena people were farmers and built burial mounds. The Hopewell people followed them.

Anasazi   The Anasazi lived in the southwestern part of what is now the United States in New Mexico, Arizona, Utah, and Colorado. Their culture flourished from about 350 B.C. to

A.D. 1450. They are thought to be the ancestors of modern Pueblo people.

Aztec (Mexica)   The Aztec moved into the Valley of Mexico from the north in about A.D. 1100. Their culture followed that of the Toltec in the region. By 1350 they had expanded their empire and became the dominant state in what became central Mexico. They were the powerful group in that area when the Spaniards arrived. At its largest, the main Aztec city of Tenochtitlán had about 250,000 residents.

Chalchihuite   The Chalchihuite people entered what is now the Sierra Madre of Mexico between A.D. 900 and 1250. They were colonized by the Aztec after the Aztec Empire rose to power. They lived in what was considered the northern frontier of the Aztec Empire.

Chavin   Chavin culture flourished in the fertile river valleys of what is now Peru from about 1000 B.C. to about 200 B.C. The Chavin lived about 1,200 to 2,000 years before the Inca Empire was established.

Chimu   The Chimu civilization lasted from 1100 A.D. to the mid-1400s in what is now Peru. The Chimu state was conquered by the Inca.

Chinchorro   The Chinchorro culture, on the coast of what is now Peru, began in about 5000 B.C. It reached its peak in about 3000 B.C. The Chinchorro are best known for the elaborate ways in which they mummified their dead. They are one of the most ancient cultures to have lived in the region.

Hohokam   The Hohokam culture arose in what is now central and southern Arizona in about 300 B.C. Hohokam people are thought to be the ancestors of the Akimel O'odham (Pima) and the Tohono O'odham (Papago). The Hohokam lived in the Southwest in the same time period as the Anasazi. Their settlements were south of those of the Anasazi.

Hopewell   Hopewell culture arose along the valleys of the Mississippi and Ohio Rivers in about 300 B.C. The Hopewell are considered part of the Mound Builders, along with the Adena people who came before them. They built huge earthworks and flourished until about A.D. 700. They were followed by the Mississippian Culture.

Inca   The Inca established an empire in what is now Peru in about A.D. 1000 and rapidly expanded it. This empire extended from what is now northwest Argentina to parts of what is now Colombia. The Inca Empire was in power when the Spanish conquistador Francisco Pizarro arrived in South America.

Iroquois League (Haudenosaunee)   The Iroquois League, or Haudenosaunee, was an alliance of Northeast tribes established some time between A.D. 1000 and 1400. The tribes included the Oneida, Mohawk, Cayuga, Onondaga, Seneca, and later the Tuscarora.

Maya   The Maya civilization arose in what is now the Yucatán Peninsula of Mexico starting in about 1500 B.C. They did not have a centralized government but instead formed city-states. Maya people also lived in what are now Belize, Guatemala, El Salvador, and Honduras. When the Aztec expanded their empire, they began collecting taxes from the Maya and demanded loyalty to the Aztec Emperor.

Mississippian Culture   The Mississippian Culture arose in about A.D. 1000. Sometimes these people are called temple mound builders. Unlike the Adena and Hopewell people, they built earthworks for temples and ceremonial centers, rather than for burials. They built Cahokia, a city of about 30,000 people, near what is St. Louis, Missouri, today. Mississippian Culture started to weaken in the 1500s, but early French explorers encountered some temple mound builders in the late 1600s.

Mixtec   The Mixtec lived in what is now southern Mexico. Their culture arose in about A.D. 900. The Aztec Empire eventually dominated the Mixtec city-states, but their culture continued to thrive until the arrival of the Spaniards.

Moche   The Moche culture arose on the northern coast of what is now Peru in about 200 B.C. It flourished until about A.D. 600. The Moche were master artists.

Mound Builders   These were American Indians of several cultures who lived in the Mississippi and Ohio River Valleys over a period of time. Some Mound Builders also lived in the Southeast. These people of the Adena, Hopewell, and Mississippian cultures built extensive earthworks.

Nazca   The Nazca people lived in the lowlands of what is now Peru. Their culture arose starting in about 600 B.C. and lasted until about A.D. 900. Later the area where they lived became part of the Inca Empire.

Old Copper Culture   Peoples who lived from about 4000 B.C. to 1500 B.C. in the Great Lakes region of North America. These Indians worked with copper deposits that were close to the surface of the Earth. They made some of the earliest metal tools and objects in the world.

Olmec   The Olmec culture flourished starting in about 1700 B.C. in the coastal lowlands of what is now Mexico. It lasted until about 400 B.C. The Olmec built several cities, including La Venta, which had a population of about 18,000. The Olmec are also known as the Rubber People because they made items from rubber.

Paracas   The Paracas culture arose in the river valleys of what is now Peru in about 1300 B.C. and flourished until about A.D. 20. Paracas people invented many weaving and pottery techniques. A thousand years later, the area where they lived became part of the Inca Empire.

Paleo-Indians   A general term for those who lived before about 4000 B.C. They were the oldest peoples of the Americas. They hunted for their food, killing large mammals, such as the wooly mammoth and the mastodon.

Poverty Point Culture   The people of Poverty Point lived in the Lower Mississippi Valley between 1730 and 1350 B.C. They are a small, distinct group within Mississippian, or Mound Building, Culture.

Teotihuacán   The Teotihuacán culture flourished in the central valley of what is now Mexico from about 1000 B.C. to 900 A.D. At its center was the city-state of Teotihuacán, which was at its strongest from about A.D. 1 to about 650. In A.D. 500 the city was home to between 100,000 and 200,000 people.

Thule   The Thule culture arose in what is now northwestern Alaska between 1,000 and 2,000 years ago. Then it spread to Greenland. Thule people were the ancestors of the Inuit. They are known for their tool-making ability.

Toltec   The Toltec migrated into what is now known as the Valley of Mexico in central Mexico in about A.D. 800. They established their capital at Tula in about 900. About 60,000 people lived in Tula. The Toltec rule lasted until some time in the

1100s, when invading groups attacked and overthrew them. Little is known about the Toltec because the Aztec used the ruins of Tula as a source of building materials for their own monuments.

Zapotec   The Zapotec established a city-state south of the Mixtec in what is now southern Mexico. In about 500 B.C. they began building the city of Monte Albán. By A.D. 450, more than 15,000 people lived in Monte Albán. Later this grew to 25,000 people. By about 700 A.D. the Zapotec began moving away from their city. Although their culture remained, the Zapotec no longer had a city-state.

TRIBES ORGANIZED BY CULTURE AREA

North American Culture Areas

ARCTIC CULTURE AREA
Aleut
Inuit

CALIFORNIA CULTURE AREA
Achomawi (Pit River)
Akwaala
Alliklik (Tataviam)
Atsugewi (Pit River)
Bear River
Cahto (Kato)
Cahuilla
Chilula
Chimariko
Chumash
Costanoan (Ohlone)
Cupeño
Diegueño (Ipai)
Esselen
Fernandeño
Gabrieliño
Huchnom
Hupa
Ipai (Diegueño)
Juaneño
Kamia (Tipai)
Karok
Kitanemuk

Konomihu
Lassik
Luiseño
Maidu
Mattole
Miwok
Nicoleño
Nomlaki
Nongatl
Okwanuchu
Patwin (subgroup of Wintun)
Pomo
Salinas
Serrano
Shasta
Sinkyone
Tolowa (Smith River)
Tubatulabal (Kern River)
Vanyume
Wailaki
Wappo
Whilkut
Wintu (subgroup of Wintun)
Wintun
Wiyot
Yahi

Yana
Yokuts
Yuki
Yurok

GREAT BASIN CULTURE AREA
Bannock
Chemehuevi
Kawaiisu
Mono
Paiute
Panamint
Sheepeater (subgroup
of Bannock
and Shoshone)
Shoshone
Snake (subgroup of Paiute)
Ute
Washoe

GREAT PLAINS CULTURE AREA
Arapaho
Arikara
Assiniboine
Atsina (Gros Ventre)
Blackfeet
Blood (subgroup of Blackfeet)
Cheyenne
Comanche
Crow
Hidatsa
Ioway
Kaw
Kichai
Kiowa
Kiowa-Apache
Mandan
Missouria
Omaha
Osage
Otoe
Pawnee
Piegan (subgroup of Blackfeet)

Plains Cree
Plains Ojibway
Ponca
Quapaw
Sarcee
Sioux (Dakota, Lakota, Nakota)
Tawakoni
Tawehash
Tonkawa
Waco
Wichita
Yscani

NORTHEAST CULTURE AREA
Abenaki
Algonkin
Amikwa (Otter)
Cayuga
Chippewa (Ojibway,
Anishinabe)
Chowanoc
Conoy
Coree (Coranine)
Erie
Fox (Mesquaki)
Hatteras
Honniasont
Huron (Wyandot)
Illinois
Iroquois (Haudenosaunee)
Kickapoo
Kitchigami
Lenni Lenape (Delaware)
Machapunga
Mahican
Maliseet
Manhattan (subgroup of Lenni
Lenape or Wappinger)
Massachuset
Mattabesac
Meherrin
Menominee
Miami

Micmac
Mingo (subgroup of Iroquois)
Mohawk
Mohegan
Montauk
Moratok
Nanticoke
Narragansett
Nauset
Neusiok
Neutral (Attiwandaronk)
Niantic
Nipmuc
Noquet
Nottaway
Oneida
Onondaga
Ottawa
Otter (Amikwa)
Pamlico (Pomeiok)
Passamaquoddy
Paugussett
Penacook
Penobscot
Pequot
Pocomtuc
Poospatuck
(subgroup of Montauk)
Potawatomi
Powhatan
Raritan
(subgroup of Lenni Lenape)
Roanoke
Sac
Sakonnet
Secotan
Seneca
Shawnee
Shinnecock
(subgroup of Montauk)
Susquehannock
Tobacco (Petun)

Tuscarora
Wampanoag
Wappinger
Weapemeoc
Wenro
Winnebago (Ho-Chunk)

**NORTHWEST COAST
CULTURE AREA**
Ahantchuyuk
Alsea
Atfalati
Bella Coola
Cathlamet
Cathlapotle
Chastacosta
Chehalis
Chelamela
Chepenafa (Mary's River)
Chetco
Chilluckittequaw
Chimakum
Chinook
Clackamas
Clallam
Clatskanie
Clatsop
Clowwewalla
Comox
Coos
Coquille (Mishikhwutmetunne)
Cowichan
Cowlitz
Dakubetede
Duwamish
Gitskan
Haida
Haisla
Heiltsuk
Kalapuya
Kuitsh
Kwakiutl

Kwalhioqua
Latgawa
Luckiamute
Lumni
Makah
Miluk
Muckleshoot
Multomah (Wappato)
Nanaimo
Nisga
Nisqually
Nooksack
Nootka
Puntlatch
Puyallup
Quaitso (Queets)
Quileute
Quinault
Rogue
Sahehwamish
Samish
Santiam
Seechelt
Semiahmoo
Siletz
Siuslaw
Skagit
Skilloot
Skykomish
Snohomish
Snoqualmie
Songish
Squamish
Squaxon (Squaxin)
Stalo
Swallah
Swinomish
Takelma (Rogue)
Taltushtuntude
Tillamook
Tlingit
Tsimshian

Tututni (Rogue)
Twana
Umpqua
Wappato (Multomah)
Wasco
Watlala (Cascade)
Yamel
Yaquina
Yoncalla

PLATEAU CULTURE AREA

Cayuse
Chelan
Coeur d'Alene
Columbia (Sinkiuse)
Colville
Entiat
Flathead (Salish)
Kalispel
Klamath
Klickitat
Kootenai (Flathead)
Lake (Senijextee)
Lillooet
Methow
Modoc
Molalla
Nez Perce
Ntlakyapamuk (Thompson)
Okanagan
Palouse
Pshwanwapam
Sanpoil
Shuswap
Sinkaietk
Sinkakaius
Skin (Tapanash)
Spokan
Stuwihamuk
Taidnapam
Tenino
Tyigh

Umatilla
Walla Walla
Wanapam
Wauyukma
Wenatchee
Wishram
Yakama

SOUTHEAST CULTURE AREA
Acolapissa
Adai
Ais
Akokisa
Alabama
Amacano
Apalachee
Apalachicola
Atakapa
Avoyel
Bayogoula
Bidai
Biloxi
Caddo
Calusa
Caparaz
Cape Fear
Catawba
Chakchiuma
Chatot
Chawasha (subgroup
of Chitimacha)
Cheraw (Sara)
Cherokee
Chiaha
Chickasaw
Chine
Chitimacha
Choctaw
Congaree
Coushatta
Creek
Cusabo
Deadose

Eno
Eyeish (Ayish)
Griga
Guacata
Guale
Hitchiti
Houma
Ibitoupa
Jeaga
Kaskinampo
Keyauwee
Koroa
Lumbee
Manahoac
Miccosukee
(subgroup of Seminole)
Mobile
Monacan
Moneton
Muklasa
Nahyssan
Napochi
Natchez
Occaneechi
Oconee
Ofo
Okelousa
Okmulgee
Opelousa
Osochi
Pasacagoula
Patiri
Pawokti
Pee Dee
Pensacola
Quinipissa
Santee (Issati)
Saponi
Sawokli
Seminole
Sewee
Shakori
Sissipahaw

Sugeree
Taensa
Tamathli
Tangipahoa
Taposa
Tawasa
Tekesta
Timucua
Tiou
Tohome
Tunica
Tuskegee
Tutelo
Waccamaw
Washa (subgroup of
  Chitimacha)
Wateree
Waxhaw
Winyaw
Woccon
Yadkin
Yamasee
Yazoo
Yuchi

SOUTHWEST CULTURE AREA

Akimel O'odham (Pima)
Apache
Coahuiltec
Cocopah
Halchidhoma
Halyikwamai
Havasupai
Hopi
Hualapai
Jumano (Shuman)
Karankawa
Keres (Pueblo Indians)
Kohuana
Maricopa
Mojave
Navajo (Dineh)
Piro (Pueblo Indians)

Pueblo
Quenchan (Yuma)
Shuman (Jumano)
Sobaipuri
Tewa (Pueblo Indians)
Tiwa (Pueblo Indians)
Tohono O'odham (Papago)
Towa (Jemez, Pueblo Indians)
Yaqui
Yavapai
Yuma (Quechan)
Zuni

SUBARCTIC CULTURE AREA

Ahtena (Copper)
Beaver (Tsattine)
Beothuk
Carrier
Chilcotin
Chipewyan
Cree
Dogrib
Eyak
Han
Hare (Kawchottine)
Ingalik
Kolchan
Koyukon
Kutchin
Montagnais
Nabesna
Nahane
Naskapi
Sekani
Slave (Slavery,
  Etchaottine)
Tahltan
Tanaina
Tanana
Tatsanottine (Yellowknife)
Tsetsaut
Tutchone (Mountain)

Mesoamerican Culture Area*

Aztec (Mexica-Nahuatl)   Olmec
Chalchiuites   Toltec
Maya   Zapotec
Mixtec

Circum-Caribbean Culture Area
(West Indies and Portion of Central America)

Arawak   Matagalpa
Boruca   Mosquito
Carib   Paya
Ciboney   Rama
Ciguayo   Silam
Coiba   Sumo
Corobici   Taino
Cuna   Talamanca
Guaymi   Ulva
Guetar   Voto
Jicaque   Yosco
Lucayo

South American Culture Areas*

ANDEAN CULTURE AREA
Achuari
Aguaruna
Chavin
Chimu
Inca
Jivaro
Mapuche
Moche
Nazca
Quecha

**CENTRAL AND
SOUTHERN CULTURE AREA**
Guarani
Mapuche

**TROPICAL FOREST (AMAZON
BASIN) CULTURE AREA**
Arawak
Carib
Tupi

* These lists do not attempt to include all groups in the area. They do, however, include a mix of ancient and modern peoples.

Appendix
MAPS

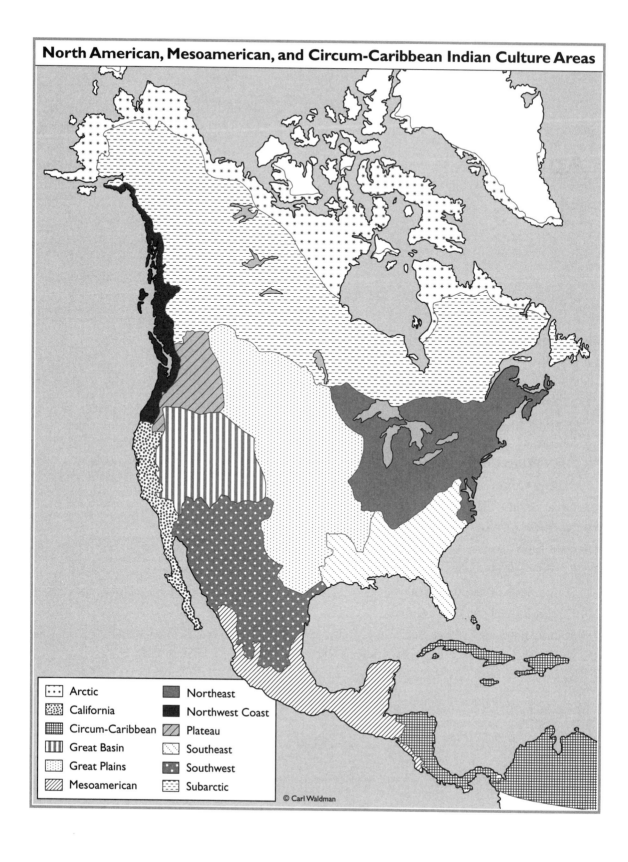

North American, Mesoamerican, and Circum-Caribbean Indian Culture Areas

Arctic

California

Circum-Caribbean

Great Basin

Great Plains

Mesoamerican

Northeast

Northwest Coast

Plateau

Southeast

Southwest

Subarctic

© Carl Waldman

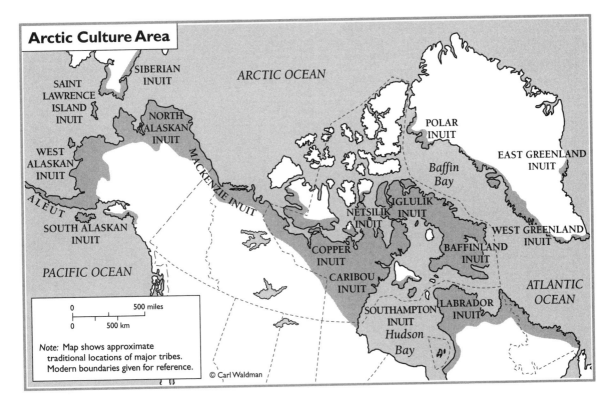

Arctic Culture Area

ARCTIC OCEAN

SIBERIAN INUIT

SAINT LAWRENCE ISLAND INUIT

WEST ALASKAN INUIT

NORTH ALASKAN INUIT

POLAR INUIT

Baffin Bay

EAST GREENLAND INUIT

ALEUT

MACKENZIE INUIT

SOUTH ALASKAN INUIT

PACIFIC OCEAN

NETSILIK INUIT

IGLULIK INUIT

COPPER INUIT

BAFFINLAND INUIT

WEST GREENLAND INUIT

CARIBOU INUIT

SOUTHAMPTON INUIT

LABRADOR INUIT

ATLANTIC OCEAN

Hudson Bay

0   500 miles
0   500 km

Note: Map shows approximate traditional locations of major tribes. Modern boundaries given for reference.

© Carl Waldman

Subarctic Culture Area

ARCTIC OCEAN

KOYUKON

INGALIK

TANANA

TANAINA

KUTCHIN

HAN

HARE

NABESNA

AHTENA

TUTCHONE

TAGISH

TATSANOTTINE

DOGRIB

TAHLTAN

NAHANE

TSETSAUT

SLAVE

CHIPEWYAN

Hudson Bay

SEKANI

CARRIER

BEAVER

THOMPSON

CHILCOTIN

WESTERN WOODS CREE

SWAMPY CREE

WEST MAIN CREE

EAST MAIN CREE

NASKAPI

MONTAGNAIS

BEOTHUK

CHIPPEWA

ALGONKIN

TÊTE DE BOULE CREE

PACIFIC OCEAN

ATLANTIC OCEAN

0   500 miles
0   500 km

Note: Map shows approximate traditional locations of major tribes. Modern boundaries given for reference.

© Carl Waldman

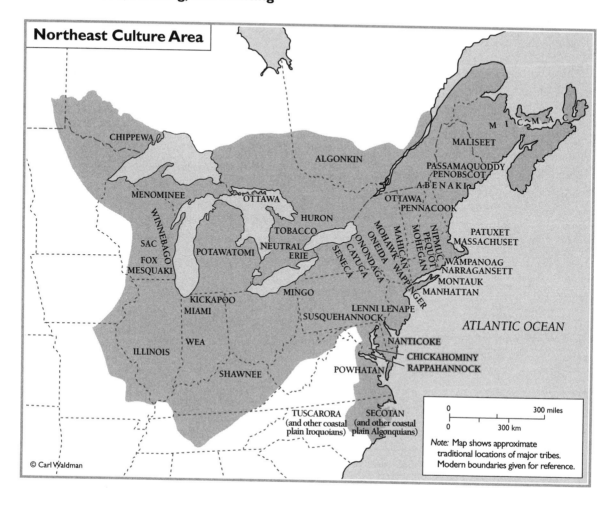

Northeast Culture Area

CHIPPEWA

ALGONKIN

M I C M A C

MALISEET

MENOMINEE

OTTAWA

PASSAMAQUODDY
PENOBSCOT
A B E N A K I

WINNEBAGO

HURON

OTTAWA
PENNACOOK

TOBACCO

SAC

NEUTRAL
ERIE

POTAWATOMI

ONEIDA
ONONDAGA
CAYUGA
SENECA

MOHAWK
MAHICAN
WAPPINGER
MOHEGAN
PEQUOT

NIPMUC

PATUXET
MASSACHUSET

FOX
MESQUAKI

WAMPANOAG
NARRAGANSETT

KICKAPOO

MINGO

MONTAUK
MANHATTAN

MIAMI

SUSQUEHANNOCK

LENNI LENAPE

ATLANTIC OCEAN

WEA

ILLINOIS

NANTICOKE

CHICKAHOMINY
RAPPAHANNOCK

SHAWNEE

POWHATAN

TUSCARORA
(and other coastal
plain Iroquoians)

SECOTAN
(and other coastal
plain Algonquians)

0   300 miles

0   300 km

Note: Map shows approximate
traditional locations of major tribes.
Modern boundaries given for reference.

© Carl Waldman

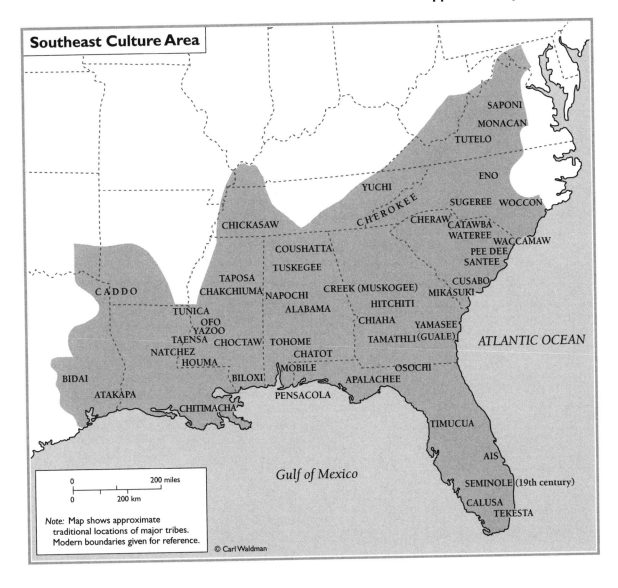

Southeast Culture Area

SAPONI
MONACAN
TUTELO
ENO
YUCHI
SUGEREE WOCCON
CHEROKEE
CHERAW CATAWBA
CHICKASAW WATEREE WACCAMAW
PEE DEE
COUSHATTA SANTEE
TUSKEGEE CUSABO
TAPOSA CREEK (MUSKOGEE) MIKASUKI
CHAKCHIUMA NAPOCHI HITCHITI
CADDO ALABAMA
TUNICA CHIAHA YAMASEE
OFO TAMATHLI (GUALE) ATLANTIC OCEAN
YAZOO CHOCTAW TOHOME
TAENSA CHATOT
NATCHEZ OSOCHI
HOUMA MOBILE
BIDAI BILOXI APALACHEE
ATAKAPA PENSACOLA
CHITIMACHA
TIMUCUA

AIS
Gulf of Mexico SEMINOLE (19th century)
CALUSA
TEKESTA

0   200 miles
0   200 km

Note: Map shows approximate
traditional locations of major tribes.
Modern boundaries given for reference.
© Carl Waldman

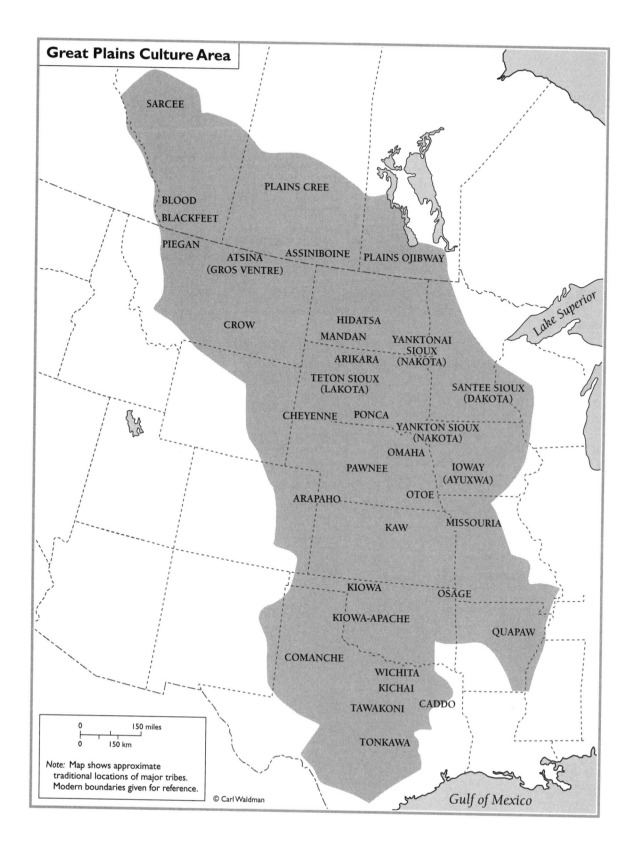

Great Plains Culture Area

SARCEE

PLAINS CREE

BLOOD
BLACKFEET
PIEGAN
ATSINA
(GROS VENTRE)
ASSINIBOINE
PLAINS OJIBWAY

CROW

HIDATSA
MANDAN
YANKTONAI
SIOUX
(NAKOTA)
ARIKARA
TETON SIOUX
(LAKOTA)
SANTEE SIOUX
(DAKOTA)
CHEYENNE
PONCA
YANKTON SIOUX
(NAKOTA)
OMAHA
PAWNEE
IOWAY
(AYUXWA)
ARAPAHO
OTOE
KAW
MISSOURIA

KIOWA
OSAGE
KIOWA-APACHE
QUAPAW
COMANCHE
WICHITA
KICHAI
CADDO
TAWAKONI
TONKAWA

Lake Superior

Gulf of Mexico

0   150 miles
0   150 km

Note: Map shows approximate
traditional locations of major tribes.
Modern boundaries given for reference.

© Carl Waldman

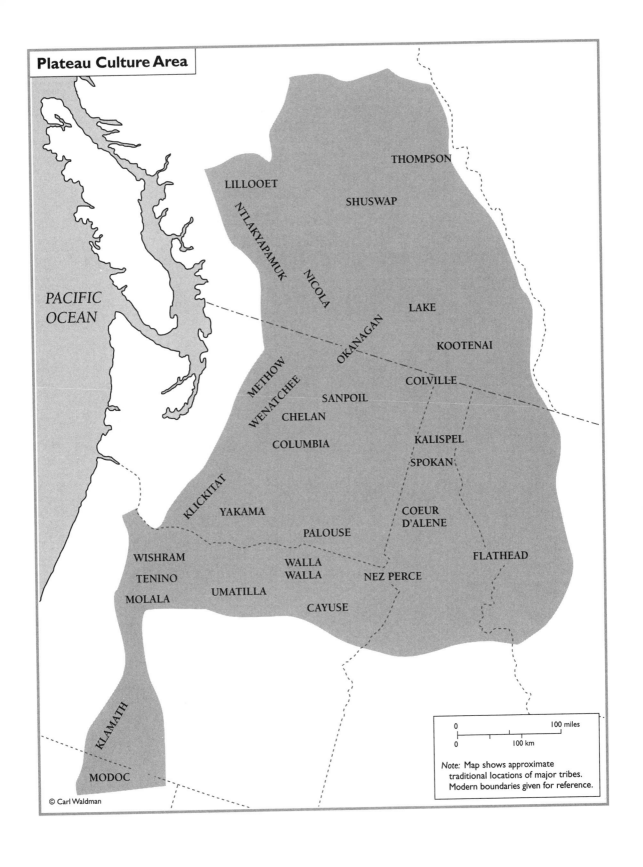

Plateau Culture Area

PACIFIC
OCEAN

THOMPSON

LILLOOET

NTLAKYAPAMUK

SHUSWAP

NICOLA

LAKE

OKANAGAN

KOOTENAI

METHOW

COLVILLE

WENATCHEE

SANPOIL

CHELAN

KALISPEL

COLUMBIA

SPOKAN

KLICKITAT

YAKAMA

COEUR
D'ALENE

PALOUSE

WISHRAM

WALLA
WALLA

FLATHEAD

TENINO

NEZ PERCE

MOLALA

UMATILLA

CAYUSE

KLAMATH

MODOC

0   100 miles

0   100 km

Note: Map shows approximate
traditional locations of major tribes.
Modern boundaries given for reference.

© Carl Waldman

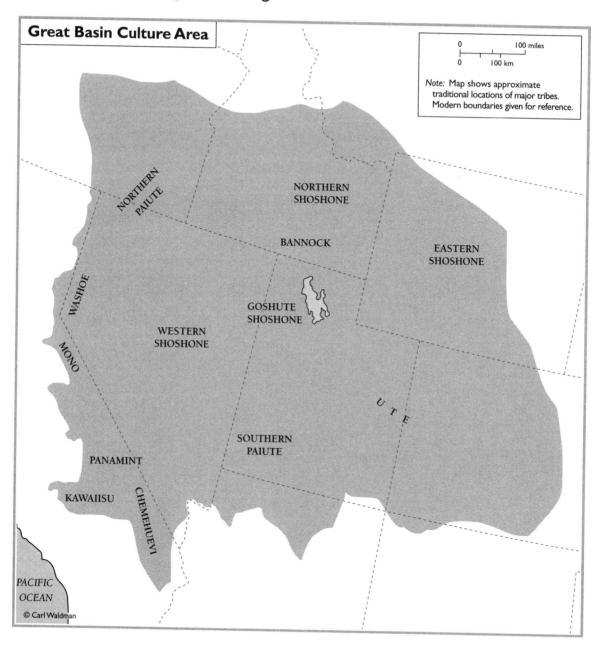

Great Basin Culture Area

0   100 miles
0   100 km

Note: Map shows approximate traditional locations of major tribes. Modern boundaries given for reference.

NORTHERN PAIUTE

NORTHERN SHOSHONE

BANNOCK

EASTERN SHOSHONE

WASHOE

GOSHUTE SHOSHONE

WESTERN SHOSHONE

MONO

UTE

SOUTHERN PAIUTE

PANAMINT

KAWAIISU

CHEMEHUEVI

PACIFIC OCEAN

© Carl Waldman

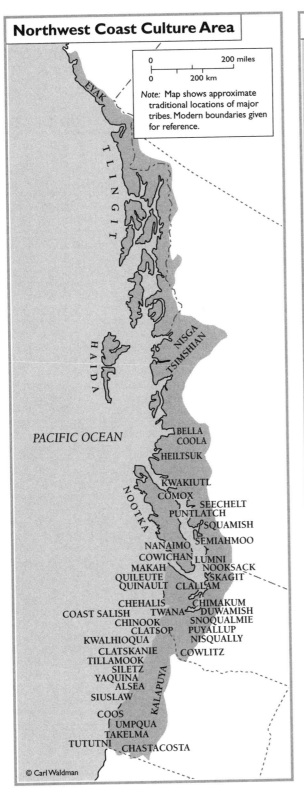

Northwest Coast Culture Area

EYAK

TLINGIT

HAIDA

NISGA
TSIMSHIAN

PACIFIC OCEAN

BELLA
COOLA

HEILTSUK

KWAKIUTL
COMOX
SEECHELT
PUNTLATCH
SQUAMISH
NANAIMO
SEMIAHMOO
COWICHAN
LUMNI
NOOKSACK
MAKAH
QUILEUTE
SKAGIT
QUINAULT
CLALLAM
CHEHALIS
CHIMAKUM
COAST SALISH TWANA DUWAMISH
CHINOOK SNOQUALMIE
CLATSOP PUYALLUP
KWALHIOQUA NISQUALLY
CLATSKANIE COWLITZ
TILLAMOOK
SILETZ
YAQUINA
ALSEA
SIUSLAW
COOS
UMPQUA
TAKELMA
TUTUTNI CHASTACOSTA

NOOTKA

KALAPUYA

© Carl Waldman

0 ———— 200 miles
0 ———— 200 km

Note: Map shows approximate
traditional locations of major
tribes. Modern boundaries given
for reference.

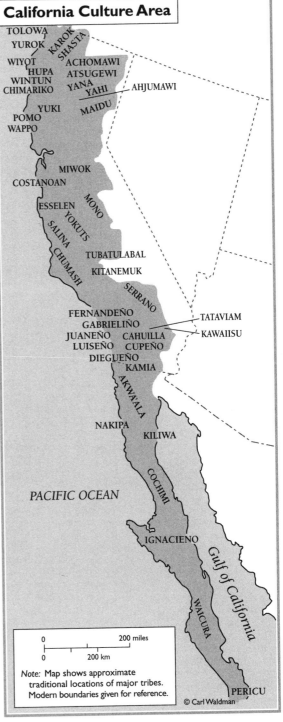

California Culture Area

TOLOWA
YUROK
KAROK
SHASTA
WIYOT
ACHOMAWI
HUPA
ATSUGEWI
WINTUN
YANA
CHIMARIKO
YAHI
AHJUMAWI
YUKI
MAIDU
POMO
WAPPO

MIWOK
COSTANOAN

ESSELEN
MONO
YOKUTS
SALINA
TUBATULABAL
CHUMASH
KITANEMUK

SERRANO

FERNANDEÑO
TATAVIAM
GABRIELIÑO
KAWAIISU
JUANEÑO
CAHUILLA
LUISEÑO
CUPEÑO
DIEGUEÑO
KAMIA

AKWA'ALA

NAKIPA
KILIWA

PACIFIC OCEAN

COCHIMI

IGNACIENO

Gulf of California

WAICURA

PERICU

0 ———— 200 miles
0 ———— 200 km

Note: Map shows approximate
traditional locations of major tribes.
Modern boundaries given for reference.
© Carl Waldman

Southwest Culture Area

HUALAPAI

HAVASUPAI

HOPI

MOJAVE

NAVAJO

JICARILLA
APACHE

HALCHIDHOMA

TIWA

YAVAPAI

TOWA   TEWA

MARICOPA

ZUNI

PECOS

YUMA

KERES

COCOPAH

PIRO

TIWA

WESTERN
APACHE

TOHONO
O'ODHAM

MIMBRENO
APACHE

CHIRICAHUA
APACHE

MESCALERO
APACHE

AKIMEL
O'ODHAM

SUMA

OPATA

JUMANO

SERI

CAHITA   JOVA

CONCHO

LIPAN
APACHE

YAQUI

TEPAHUE

TARAHUMARA

KARANKAWA

VAVROHIO

MAYO

TOBOSO

ZOE

COMANITO

NIO

COAHUILTEC

LAGUNERO

GUASAVE

TEPEHUAN

ZACATEC

BOCALOS

JANAMBRE

PISONES

NEGRITO

TAMAULIPEC

*Gulf
of
Mexico*

HUICHOL

PACIFIC OCEAN

TEPECANO

GUACHICHIL

JONAZ

COLOTLAN

GUAMARES

TEUL

PAME

Gulf of California

0   150 miles

0   150 km

Note: Map shows approximate
traditional locations of major tribes.
Modern boundaries given for reference.

© Carl Waldman

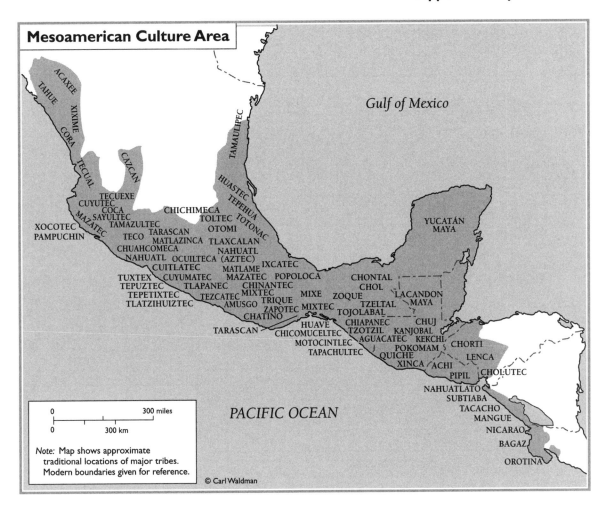

Mesoamerican Culture Area

Gulf of Mexico

ACAXEE
TAHUE
XIXIME
CORA
TECUAL
CAZCAN
TAMAULIPEC

TECUEXE
CUYUTEC
COCA
SAYULTEC
CHICHIMECA
HUASTEC
TEPEHUA
XOCOTEC
PAMPUCHIN
MAZATEC
TAMAZULTEC
TARASCAN
OTOMI
TOLTEC
TOTONAC
YUCATÁN
MAYA
TECO
MATLAZINCA
TLAXCALAN
CHUAHCOMECA
NAHUATL
NAHUATL OCUILTECA (AZTEC)
CUITLATEC
MATLAME
IXCATEC
TUXTEX CUYUMATEC
MAZATEC POPOLOCA
CHONTAL
TEPUZTEC
TLAPANEC
CHINANTEC
CHOL
LACANDON
TEPETIXTEC
MIXTEC
MIXE
ZOQUE
MAYA
TLATZIHUIZTEC
TEZCATEC
AMUSGO TRIQUE
ZAPOTEC MIXTEC
TZELTAL
CHATINO
TOJOLABAL
CHUJ
TARASCAN
HUAVE
CHIAPANEC
CHICOMUCELTEC
TZOTZIL KANJOBAL
MOTOCINTLEC
AGUACATEC KEKCHI
CHORTI
TAPACHULTEC
POKOMAM
LENCA
QUICHE
XINCA ACHI
PIPIL
CHOLUTEC
NAHUATLATO
SUBTIABA
TACACHO
MANGUE
NICARAO
BAGAZ
OROTINA

PACIFIC OCEAN

0 ————————— 300 miles
0 ————————— 300 km

Note: Map shows approximate
traditional locations of major tribes.
Modern boundaries given for reference.

© Carl Waldman

Circum-Caribbean Culture Area

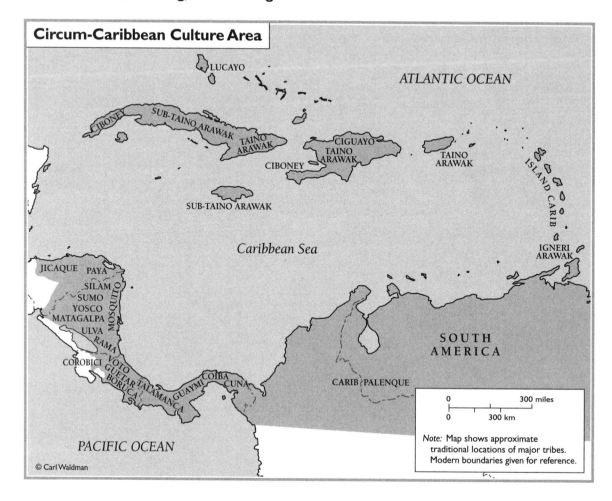

South American Culture Areas

CIRCUM-CARIBBEAN

CARIB
PALENQUE

TUPI
ARAWAK

AGUARUNA
ACHUARI
JIVARO

CARIB

ARAWAK

TUPI

CHIMU

INCA

TROPICAL FOREST

ANDEAN

EASTERN
HIGHLANDS

GUARANI

GUARANI

MAPUCHE

PAMPAS

CENTRAL AND SOUTHERN

TIERRA DEL FUEGO

ANDEAN	Culture areas
PAMPAS	Regions
MAPUCHE	Tribes and peoples
——	Approximate culture area boundaries
··········	Approximate regional boundaries

0   800 miles
0   800 km

Note: See the Circum-Caribbean map for the entire scope of the culture area.

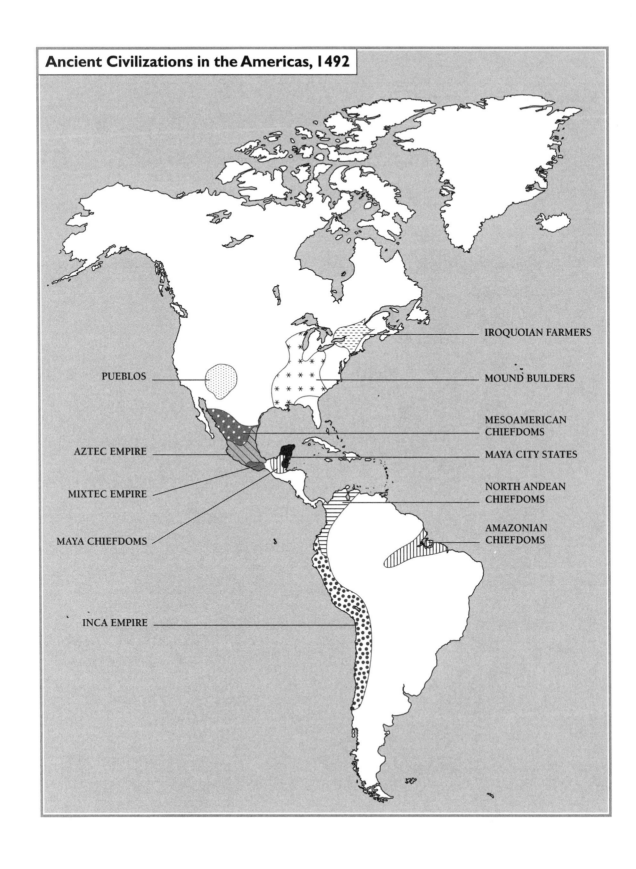

Ancient Civilizations in the Americas, 1492

IROQUOIAN FARMERS

PUEBLOS

MOUND BUILDERS

MESOAMERICAN
CHIEFDOMS

AZTEC EMPIRE

MAYA CITY STATES

MIXTEC EMPIRE

NORTH ANDEAN
CHIEFDOMS

MAYA CHIEFDOMS

AMAZONIAN
CHIEFDOMS

INCA EMPIRE

FURTHER READING

Brown, Fern G. *American Indian Science: A New Look at Old Cultures.* New York: Twenty-First-Century Books/Henry Holt and Co., 1997.

Bruchac, Joseph, and Michael Caduto. *Native Plant Stories.* Golden, Colo.: Fulcrum Publishing, 1995.

Carrasco, David. *Daily Life of the Aztecs: Keepers of the Sun and Moon.* Westport, Conn.: Greenwood Press, 1998.

Caduto, Michael, and Joseph Bruchac. *Native American Gardening: Stories, Projects and Recipes for Families.* Golden, Colo.: Fulcrum Publishing, 1996.

Cox, Beverly. *Spirit of the Harvest: North American Indian Cooking.* New York: Stewart, Tabori & Chang, 1991.

Dennee, Joanne, Jack Peduzzi, Julia Hand, and Carolyn Peduzzi. *In the Three Sisters Garden: Native American Traditions, Myths, and Culture Around the Theme of the Garden: Common Roots Guidebook.* Montpelier, Vt.: Foods Works, 1995.

Goodchild, Peter. *Survival Skills of the North American Indians (2nd ed.).* Chicago, Ill.: Chicago Review Press, 1999.

Gunderson, Mary. *American Indian Cooking before 1500.* Mankato, Minn.: Capstone Press, 2000.

Johnson, Sylvia S. *Tomatoes, Potatoes, Corn and Beans: How Foods of the America Changed Eating around the World.* New York: Atheneum, 1997.

Keoke, Emory, and Kay Marie Porterfield. *The Encyclopedia of American Indian Contributions to the World: 15,000 Years of Inventions and Innovation.* New York: Facts On File, Inc., 2002.

Kimball, Yeffe, Jean Anderson, and Gary Soucie. *The Art of American Indian Cooking: Over 150 Delicious, Authentic and Traditional Dishes from Five North American Regions.* Guilford, Conn.: Lyons Press, 2000.

Liptak, Karen. *North American Indian Survival Skills.* New York: Franklin Watts, 1990.

Malpass, Michael A. *Daily Life in the Inca Empire.* Westport, Conn.: Greenwood Press, 2002.

Montgomery, David. *Native American Crafts and Skills: A Fully Illustrated Guide to Wilderness Living and Survival.* Guilford, Conn.: Lyons Press, 2000.

Murdoch, David. *Eyewitness: North American Indians.* New York: DK Publishers, 2000.

Sharer, Robert J. *Daily Life in Maya Civilization.* Westport, Conn.: Greenwood Press, 2002.

Wilson, Gilbert L. *Buffalo Bird Woman's Garden: As Told to Gilbert L. Wilson.* St. Paul: Minnesota Historical Society Press, 1987.

Wolfson, Evelyn. *From Abenaki to Zuni: A Dictionary of Native American Tribes.* New York: Walker Publishing Co., 1988.

Wood, Marian. *Ancient America: Cultural Atlas for Young People, Revised Edition.* New York: Facts On File, 2003.

INDEX

Page numbers in *italics* indicate photographs. Page numbers in **boldface** indicate box features. Page numbers followed by *m* indicate maps. Page numbers followed by *g* indicate glossary entries. Page numbers followed by *t* indicate time line entries.